The Technique
of the Love Affair

It's incongruous to find the cold word "technique" applied to something
as volatile and irrational as a love affair. Yet for Doris Langley Moore,
there's a method in the madness of desire. The affair is a work of art,
the result of a union between constraint and fancy. In his memoir,
The Sweet and Twenties (1958), Beverley Nichols recalls the time
when amorous adventures were conducted "with elegance
and refinement." Moore would have agreed. Moreover,
unlike other manuals addressed to the single woman,
The Technique assiduously avoids moral
posturing, appealing mainly to good
taste and common sense.

■

by a Gentlewoman
Afraid of scandalizing her new in-laws, Moore disguised her identity.
She would write decades later, "Nowadays it would be considered
suitable for readings at the Y.W.C.A." By the third edition,
in 1936, her full name appeared on the title page.

The Technique
of the Love Affair

BY A GENTLEWOMAN

[DORIS LANGLEY MOORE]

EDITED, WITH NOTES AND COMMENTARY, BY

Norrie Epstein

Pantheon Books   New York

All rights reserved under International and Pan-American Copyright
Conventions. Published in the United States by Pantheon Books,
a division of Random House, Inc., New York, and simultaneously
in Canada by Random House of Canada Limited, Toronto.
The original text of *The Technique of the Love Affair* was originally
published by Simon & Schuster Inc., New York, in 1928. Published by
arrangement with the Estate of Doris Langley Moore.

Library of Congress Cataloging-in-Publication Data

Moore, Doris Langley, 1902–89
The technique of the love affair / by a Gentlewoman;
edited and annotated by Norrie Epstein.
p.   cm.
"Originally published anonymously in 1928."
ISBN 0-679-44402-5
1. Courtship.   2. Love.   3. Man-woman relationships.
I. Epstein, Norrie.   II. Title.
HQ801.M75   1999
306.73′4—dc21   98-34354
CIP

Random House Web Address: www.randomhouse.com

Book design by M. Kristen Bearse

Printed in the United States of America
First Edition

2   4   6   8   9   7   5   3   1

An absence, the decline of a dinner invitation, an unintentional coldness, can accomplish more than all the cosmetics and beautiful dresses in the world.

—MARCEL PROUST

Editor's Introduction

■ ■ ■

On November 17, 1928, Dorothy Parker mentioned a new book in her column in *The New Yorker:*

> I acquired a book called *The Technique of the Love Affair,* by one who signs herself "A Gentlewoman," and set out to learn how to loop the usual Dancing Men. I have thought, in times past, that I had been depressed. I have regarded myself as one who had walked hand-in-hand with sadness. But until I read that book, depression, as I knew it, was still in its infancy. I have found out, from its pages, that never once have I been right. Never once. Not even one little time.
>
> You know how you ought to be with men? You should always be aloof, you should never let them know you like them, you must on no account let them feel that they are of any importance to you, you must be wrapped up in your own concerns, you may never let them lose sight of the fact that you are superior, you must be, in

short, a regular stuffed chemise. And if you could see what I've been doing!

The Technique of the Love Affair makes, I am bitterly afraid, considerable sense. If only it had been written and placed in my hands years ago, maybe I could have been successful instead of just successive.

That Dorothy Parker should review a book called *The Technique of the Love Affair* is, like one of her own stories, both sad and funny. It is also fitting. Published in England, where it had caused a scandal two years earlier, *The Technique* was addressed to women like Mrs. Parker who had never once been right.

Its readers were the so-called New Women who emerged during World War I. The subject of cartoons in *The New Yorker* and *Punch,* the typical modern woman lived in a bachelor flat in the city; she earned her own living and believed in "sexual freedom" (although she might not have known exactly what that meant). She smoked cigarettes, drank cocktails, and swore in public. She even looked different: Slim and uncorseted, she wore her skirts short and her hair bobbed. To all appearances, she was physically, legally, and emotionally emancipated. The generation gap between the woman of the 1920s and her Victorian mother was all but unbridgeable, and a girl could no longer look to her elders for advice.

The Technique is a guide for the modern woman written by one. The 1920s, like the 1960s, was an era in which youth set the standard, so it wasn't surprising that the anonymous

"Gentlewoman" turned out to be a twenty-three-year–old sophisticate named Doris Langley Moore.

In one generation the Byzantine rituals of Victorian courtship had undergone a revolution: single women no longer extended invitations to suitors to "call" or held "at homes." Now even respectable women went unchaperoned to nightclubs, restaurants, and movies. The modern date was born, and the once neutral telephone became an instrument of both despair and bliss.

Moore's guidebook navigates women through terra incognita, a social world in which the old rules were no longer valid. Surely, it must be one of the first manuals to claim that a woman should cultivate more than one suitor and to dismiss virtue, intelligence, and domestic skill as irrelevant.

In its mood, style, and tone, *The Technique* evokes the postwar sensibility as portrayed by Noël Coward and Evelyn Waugh, in which Champagne, party games, and romantic intrigues were *de rigueur*. It was a time when men and women had dalliances or affairs, not relationships. Cypria and Saccharissa, the two women whose voices we hear throughout *The Technique,* could almost be characters in a Shavian drawing-room comedy. An undercurrent of irony runs through the book—the author refuses to take anything too seriously, including her own advice. This was an age in which it was important *not* to be earnest; flippancy and cynicism were sane responses to an insane war.

The effects of the "Great War" are felt throughout *The Technique*. In the first chapter, the women allude to its casualties: the loss of ideals such as honor or virtue, and a diminishment of "older values," such as "money, birth, rank and respectability." The experienced Cypria doesn't lament the passing of the old ways, but for her and other young women, wartime casualties meant a shortage of eligible men. When there aren't enough men to go around, a woman needs a strategy to give her an edge over the competition.

The Technique of the Love Affair is a self-help book that transcends the genre. Written in dialogue, it's a droll parody of Plato's *Symposium*. Like Plato's Diotima, Cypria (whose name derives from Venus's birthplace) is an expert in the art of love. Her pupil is the aptly named Saccharissa, a naïf who accepts the illusions of the past. In the course of the dialogue, Cypria will demolish her most cherished beliefs. "You don't believe what you don't wish to believe," she tells her. Women, no matter what they think, are not emancipated, for they still need men, "morally, physically, socially, and financially." Men, however, "rarely need women, and most never think of marrying unless they are attached." Yet, with ingenuity, artifice, and "prestige" (Moore's word for any quality that makes a woman desirable), most women can captivate a man and retain his love.

Saccharissa is appalled. "But Cypria, this is atrocious! To say we can actually make men love us— love us by these horrible methods! I am no moralist, but your cynicism has shocked me." Yet, with her sophist arguments, the seductress convinces her—and us—of the need for guile; by the end of the book, the enlightened Saccharrisa is eager to try out Cypria's technique.

Since Moore is concerned with the *technique* of the

affair, and not the joys of "True Love," her views are pragmatic, at times Machiavellian. Like it or not, this is the
Realpolitik of romance:

One of the most painful lessons the virtuous have to
learn is that people do not fall in love with virtue. A
noble character may enhance the attractions of one
already beloved . . . but only in the rarest instance can it
in itself produce the desire for possession. . . .

Certainly [chastity] is consoling, just as the sense of
chastity is consoling to those who never had the opportunity of losing it; but subconsciously it was meant to be
provocative to men as well. . . .

Discretion, self-control, and dignity, not "intimacy" or
"communication," the much-invoked bywords of our own
age, are keys to a successful affair. In this sense, *The Technique* is an amusing and salutary contrast to the current crop
of "relationship books." Unlike contemporary self-help
gurus, the anonymous Gentlewoman assumes that women
are reasonable beings, not victims of desire.

Women today can read the *The Technique* as a period
piece, as a young woman's *jeu d'esprit,* or as a useful handbook. As Cypria says, "You may read it from whatever
point of view you please—either to be instructed or
amused." Some of Moore's advice may seem dated or silly,
perhaps even shocking. Yet, the author, an intelligent,
strong-minded woman, isn't degrading women when she
tells them to chatter or wheedle for gifts. In her own sly
way, she's mocking—and humoring—the male need to

dominate. This, she is saying, is what men expect of us. To Moore, sex roles are just that, roles to be adopted and discarded at will. But, as she points out, her technique only works with the average male whose taste is fairly predictable. (And when it comes to women, the author notes that most men are conventional.) Who then has the power? The man who believes he's superior? Or the woman who lets him think he is?

■ ■ ■

A Note on the Text

There are three types of text in this book: the original *Technique of the Love Affair* by Doris Langley Moore, my gloss in the margins, and my brief essays in the form of shaded text at the end of chapters. I have also supplied the epigraphs that open each chapter.

N.E.

The Technique
of the Love Affair

None but a woman can teach the science of herself: and though I own I am very young, a young woman may be as agreeable for a tutoress as an old one.

—MRS. INCHBALD, *Lover's Vows*

■

Mrs. Inchbald:

Known as one of the few sensible women in an age that ridiculed the follies of her sex, Mrs. Elizabeth Inchbald (1753–1821) was an actress, dramatist, novelist, and editor. Her novel *A Simple Story* has rarely been out of print since its publication in 1791.

Contents

...

One

Two

Three

Four

One

∎∎∎

We may teach our children that honesty
is the best policy, but natural selection favors
the skillful lie. In the context of courtship,
a successful deceit carries a reproductive
advantage.

—MARY BATTEN, *Sexual Strategies,* 1992

CYPRIA Women are more guileful than men, but men have the advantage of being more necessary to us than we are to them. That is the keynote of the whole position between the sexes.

SACCHARISSA I don't believe that men are more necessary to us.

CYPRIA You don't believe what you don't wish to believe. Speaking in general terms, women need men morally, physically, socially, and financially. Men's requirements of women are not usually so various.

SACCHARISSA But you talk like a Victorian. We are emancipated now.[1]

CYPRIA I am not so sure of it. At any rate, we have yet to controvert the fact that men can make shift to be happy without us, but we are really very miserable without them.

SACCHARISSA Suppose I give you that point—still, we are indispensable in our professional capacities. What do you make of that?

CYPRIA Nothing. It is no consolation to know that men must make use of us as nurses, typists, actresses, and housemaids. The question is, what is their private and personal need of us? And the answer is, very little. Women as

[1] *But you talk like a Victorian.*
  To a generation that flouted convention and prided itself on modernity, "Victorian" meant "old-fashioned." To bohemians and intellectuals it denoted moral hypocrisy and, in Bertrand Russell's words, "goody-goody priggery."

We are emancipated now.
  It took a world war to push women into the twentieth century. For the first time in modern his-

tory, they were a crucial part of the labor force, performing work vital for their country. As Nicholas Courtney points out in *In Society*, ordinary women during wartime did more to advance the cause than all the fanatics who tied themselves to lampposts (a gesture roughly equivalent to the "bra burnings" of the 1970s). In 1918, suffrage was granted to women over thirty who were homeowners (or married to one). But it wasn't until 1928 that all British women were granted the vote.

■

[2] *Women as women are a luxury . . .*
    The object of both pity and derision, a spinster was called "odd," not because she was peculiar, but because she was single in a world of pairs. In contrast, the unattached male was a prize, indispensable to hostesses who demanded even-numbered dinner parties.
    When faced with a shortage of women, men tend to take aggressive measures. Throughout the nineteenth century, marriageable females were imported *en masse* to the American West and the scarcity of eligible females in Alaska often led to the delivery of a mail-order bride, solutions unthinkable for women in any era.

women are a luxury,[2] and a luxury that, unlike most others, is too plentiful—in fact a drug on the market.

SACCHARISSA Don't forget that women are an essential part of a home and family.

CYPRIA True, but so are men. And there they still have the advantage of us; the average woman feels a craving to form a family, and the average man does it in spite of himself. In ordinary circumstances, a man does not think of marrying until he has become attached: women make plans for their wedded life almost before they have done with adolescence. I call to witness the not quite obsolete bottom drawer.[3]

SACCHARISSA Well, and if I admit our need of Man— what then?

CYPRIA Then you admit what I have often heard you deny—you admit the excuse for our guile, for it is natural that we should acquaint ourselves with all the means of getting what we cannot do without.

SACCHARISSA I am not quite clear as to what you mean by guile. Can you define it?

CYPRIA I will try. It stands, in the love affair, on the border-line between honesty and dishonesty. It is not duplicity and deceit, but dissembling and artifice; not craft but craftsmanship, not cunning but ingenuity. She who uses it may be allowed now and then an excursion into the region of candour, but she must never be lured into the insidious tangled maze that lies on the other side of the road, for though honesty is not the best policy in amatory dealings, dishonesty is certainly the worst.

SACCHARISSA But, Cypria, this is atrocious! To say

that we can actually make men love us—*love* us, by these horrible methods! I am no moralist, but your cynicism has shocked me.

CYPRIA   My dear friend, don't be a pharisee! I recommend nothing that the chastest women have not practised from earliest time. Even the tearful, trembling, blushing, impeccably virtuous heroines of Victorian literature were guileful according to my definition. Can you, in the face of all the books you see upon these shelves, deny their dissembling and their ingenuity? Can you deny that their very artlessness was a fine art? They repulsed advances they longed to encourage, and encouraged advances they seemed to repulse; in situations of the slightest embarrassment they feigned headaches and graceful swoons; they pretended to be taken unawares by avowals they had timed to a nicety; they gave nothing until they were sure of receiving all. Their charming modesty was—dare I say it?—a part of their stock-in-trade, a part so valuable that it spared them the need for many other wiles. And to be innocent, to know nothing of the world—what could be more attractive! Innocence, though there is much to be said against it, appeals to two of the strongest instincts in man—the instinct to teach and the instinct to protect. They were guileful mothers who kept their daughters innocent, and guileful daughters who allowed themselves to be kept so!

SACCHARISSA   Come, you are going too far. Do you say that even their modesty, their chastity itself, was a matter of deliberate calculation?

CYPRIA   I would say rather, subconscious calculation, if that is not too large a paradox for you. The Victorian ladies

A relatively recent parallel to feminine desperation of the 1920s is the almost hysterical reaction to *Newsweek*'s 1985 pronouncement that after thirty a woman had as much chance of finding a husband as getting attacked by a terrorist.

[3] *. . . bottom drawer.*
   The British version of the "hope chest," containing clothing and such household items that a girl collects in anticipation of married life.

[4] *There are no spinsters now-a-days . . .*

After the war, a striking new woman appeared. Variously called "flapper," *"garçonne, "* or "bachelor girl," she was a skinny, boyish creature with bobbed (or shingled) hair who smoked cigarettes, guzzled gin in jazz clubs, and delighted in scandalizing her elders with her permissive views on marriage and monogamy.

Psychiatrists studied this specimen of womanhood as if she belonged to an alien species:

The garçonne *is a new type of woman—economically independent, with a job of her own, desirous of establishing independence in her love-life too. She does not refuse marriage as a principle, but marriage is not an aim when she considers an intimate relationship with a man. How are we to account for this tendency which undoubtedly exists to-day?*

Perhaps the excess of women over men in many European countries after the War made competition much keener, so that women felt they had to offer more in accordance with the laws of supply and demand.

—Olga Knopf,
The Art of Being a Woman, 1932

lived in a period filled with soothing fictions, and we may be quite sure that they managed to believe in chastity as an end in itself, even while they were considering its market value.

SACCHARISSA   Its value has sadly diminished [*see* On Chastity *at the end of this chapter*].

CYPRIA   It has diminished—not sadly—along with other old values. Money, birth, rank, respectability—they are all worth less than they were. It was not man, but woman herself, who relegated chastity to a more reasonable position among the virtues. Far be it from me to insinuate that she has discarded it, but she no longer vaunts it as her proudest boast. It is no longer her main-stay, her protection, her chief allurement.

SACCHARISSA   And what is the substitute?

CYPRIA   The only one feasible in a country stripped by disaster of its more absurd illusions and in which our sex is greatly in the majority.

SACCHARISSA   And that is—?

CYPRIA   A well-rationalised but foolishly-handled assumption of independence. We are—so we tell everyone daily in the newspapers—independent of men, and consequently quite indifferent to them. Single women, we protest, remain so from choice; they prefer to go on living under the jurisdiction of their parents, or in business girls' hostels or poky lodgings. There are no spinsters now-a-days, only bachelor girls.[4] Men need not enter our scheme of things except as employers, employees, and dancing partners. If one of these should happen to fall in love with us, we may honour him by nominally sacrificing our independence, but as for deliberately setting out to get married, no modern, emancipated woman does that! Of course, all this is exactly the sort of fabrication one expects where the superfluous women are numbered by hundreds of thousands.

SACCHARISSA Yes, I grant that it is a fabrication, but I think we have woven it to console ourselves, and not merely as a new piece of guile to replace one which was growing threadbare.

CYPRIA Certainly it is consoling, just as the sense of chastity is consoling to those who have never had the opportunity of losing it; but subconsciously it was meant to be provocative to men as well. You know we only talk of independence where *they* can hear us. In the ladies' magazines we tell each other how to get husbands.

SACCHARISSA Well, I fail to see how we have profited by the new pose, apart from getting some comfort out of it.

CYPRIA No, we have gained very little by it. All the same, if we must take up a general attitude, this was the only one to be adopted in an era whose social conditions would make blushing modesty and shrinking innocence look a little ridiculous. Women who do man's work, play man's games, and enter into man's province in a dozen different ways, need not entirely abandon feminine delicacy (though unhappily they often do); but their dress, talk, and manners must necessarily become masculine to a certain degree. Having sacrificed so many of our furbelows to war and commerce, there is nothing to do but be piquant—provoking men to want us by pretending that we don't want them.

SACCHARISSA But it has not provoked them to want us.

After each world war, it was feared that heightened competition between women for men would lead to increased promiscuity. The spectre of loneliness encouraged some women to embrace a way of life that would have once seemed incomprehensible.

A common sight in the thirties—to be seen, for some reason, especially on railway trains—was the standard Lesbian couple in tweeds, who had come together as girls after each had lost a fiancé, lover or husband.
—Paul Fussell,
The Great War and Modern Memory, 1975

Not surprisingly, in 1928 the first serious "Lesbian novel," Radclyffe Hall's *The Well of Loneliness,* was published—and banned—in both England and America.

■

5*And even the ineligible are on a footing . . .*

To the upper crust, "eligible" was shorthand for a list of criteria, understood but rarely stated. Family, schools, clubs, friends, and finances were all taken into consideration. The question of eligibility was more crucial for women than for men: If a woman married below her social position, she descended to her husband's class; if above, she ascended.

A girl's first husband must be eligible, otherwise she will very soon go downhill altogether.
— Nancy Mitford,
Christmas Pudding, 1976

■

⁶*. . . else why so many divorces?*

In 1920, a record 3,747 divorces were granted in England. Under the laws of the day, a husband had only to prove that his wife was adulterous, but the wife had to prove *both* adultery and cruelty or desertion. Very often, a husband might "do the right thing" and supply the evidence by arranging a night in a hotel with a woman he'd hired for the purpose.

CYPRIA   No, because up till now the pretence has only been kept up in public. We have not had the strength of mind to carry it into private life. Men have never been more in demand than at the present time.

SACCHARISSA   You are right there. Any eligible youth may have more invitations than he knows how to accept.

CYPRIA   And even the ineligible are on a footing undreamed of before the war; quite young and charming women will often pay a man's way for him rather than stay at home for want of an escort.[5] We are simply defeating our own ends. It is useless to tell men we are independent, and then beg them to come and dance with us. It is fatuous to proclaim that we don't care whether we marry or not, and then fall into the arms of the first man who asks us, as countless women do—else why so many divorces?[6] We are not managing the thing skilfully. Independence will never be profitable to us as a sex: it is only as individuals that we must ride high horses.

SACCHARISSA   I don't see why we should ride high horses at all.

CYPRIA   What! After everything I have told you about man's unfair advantage over us?

SACCHARISSA   We must simply resign ourselves to the fact that we stand in the weaker position.

CYPRIA   Resign ourselves! Thank Heaven, Saccharissa, that all women are not like you, or we should still be paying men large dowries to induce them to marry us. Until woman is the absolute equal of man, in circumstances as well as in rights, we must resign ourselves to nothing. Why, consider for a moment just a few of the advantages he has in his dealings with us—his invaluable capacity for separating love from all his other avocations, his greater freedom physically and morally, his resilience, his power to recover sooner from a lapse into vice or folly, and how much more lightly his sins against convention are regarded. In short, consider that it is not his task to bear children, and that through this alone he has the superiority of position. Then, if you are entirely spiritless, you may talk of resignation. Man stands before us vain and cocksure, armed by Nature herself with weapons—he is casual, he is free, he is *necessary.* That is the point—we cannot do without him. If you will not resort to artifice in order to obtain him, you must indeed resign yourself, not to the weaker position, but to no position at all.

SACCHARISSA But can artificial weapons ever prove stronger than natural ones?

CYPRIA The spear is stronger than the claw.

SACCHARISSA You are evidently one of those who believe there is a constant warfare between the sexes.

CYPRIA There is no more war between the sexes than there is war between a mother and an unruly child. The mother wishes to control the child for its own happiness and ultimate good as well as hers. If it has been spoiled, and has grown conceited, she is obliged to rebuke its arrogance, gently or severely according to the nature of the offence. She does not punish it wantonly and heedlessly, but with deliberation and regret.

SACCHARISSA Can that analogy be sincerely drawn?

CYPRIA Why not? No woman is happy in love unless she sees the possibility of bestowing happiness on her lover; we do not make men suffer for the pleasure of seeing them

Among the fashionable set, annual rites known as "coming out" and the "Season" were designed to introduce young women to the "right sort" of man. One debutante likened the experience to being "put up for auction and to find no takers." It was an extraordinary coup to land a husband one's first season "out." The less fortunate would continue to appear until they either found a husband (usually not of the first order) or discreetly disappeared. The spinster's presence, like that of Banquo's ghost, had an unnerving effect on the newer girls.

■

[7] *Yet we dare not give rein to our generosity . . .*

The novelist Anita Brookner expresses the dilemma of a sensitive woman: the awareness that to be loved a woman must renounce the desire to be loved:

My mistake was to lie in his arms moist-eyed with tenderness and gratitude, when the correct stance would have been a certain detachment, an irony, as if to imply that he would have to love me to a much higher standard to convince me that I had to take him seriously. I should have found such a tactic odious, but now I see that it is sometimes necessary to meet withdrawal with withdrawal, dismissal with dismissal. . . . I see that if a woman had it in mind to bring a man to heel she may have to play a part which runs counter to her own instincts, unless her instincts are those of an aggressor. . . .

Brief Lives, 1990

writhe. We are innately liberal and yielding, and it is not easy for us to appear otherwise. Yet we dare not give rein to our generosity, for men, like children, soon tire of what is soon obtained.[7]

SACCHARISSA But how tiresome to be for ever suppressing one's better instincts, hiding them and keeping them in check!

CYPRIA Yes, it is irksome to be niggardly when one longs to be lavish, but one gets the knack in time. Practice makes perfect, and the game is really worth the candle. Besides, one learns to suppress one's worst instincts as well as one's best, and that is beneficial. And if one needs an unselfish motive to help one along—well, let us say we are niggardly in the beginning only to be more lavish in the end.

SACCHARISSA Do you think that any woman with a sound working knowledge of all the wiles of captivation, and the courage to employ them, would be able to attract and hold a man's love?

CYPRIA Unless she be afflicted with any dreadful abnormality of body or mind, yes.

SACCHARISSA You mean that she would require neither beauty, intellect, nor goodness?

CYPRIA If she had nothing whatsoever of those attributes, she would be dreadfully abnormal, and therefore an exception. With a moderate supply of each, however, and with presence of mind, self-control, and the guilefulness we have spoken of, she might be almost invincible.

SACCHARISSA I cannot promise to share your point of view, but I should much like to hear this guilefulness described in detail.

CYPRIA   Very well, I shall have it all set down for you, and you may read it from whatever point of view you please—either to be instructed or amused. But do not let it fall into the hands of any of your men friends, for that would be a disloyalty to your sex. If men gain possession of women's weapons they will turn them into shields for themselves.

SACCHARISSA   But I may circulate your treatise among my women friends?

CYPRIA   Certainly, and the more the merrier.

On Chastity

Its value has sadly diminished. (p. 14)
Saccharissa yearns for the security of the past, when chastity was a woman's chief glory, whereas Cypria takes a more pragmatic view. Forty years before their grand-daughters, flappers experienced all the tensions and dilemmas of the 1960s. Indeed, the postwar decade brought the first real "sexual revolution." More than any single issue, the "Sex Question" was the great generational divide.

The "New Psychology" of Sigmund Freud, which had entered the public imagination, insisted that women had instinctual drives, and implied that sex could be used for recreation as well as procreation. The division between sex for fun and sex for procreation became a reality in 1924, when Margaret Sanger opened the first birth control clinic in England, and Marie Stopes published her landmark manual on birth control, *Married Love*. With accessible contraception, more women indulged in forbidden sex—premarital and extramarital—with no one the wiser.

Among progressive thinkers, good sex was a prescription for mental health. Marital handbooks, such as Theodore Hendrik Van de Velde's *The Perfect Marriage* (1928) (for decades almost compulsory reading for engaged couples), were unprecedented in their candor; body parts, positions, and activities were described and called by their proper names, and wives were given a more active role in the sexual act.

The new clinical and scientific attitude toward sexual intercourse helped to strip chastity of its sacramental significance. Soon references to sex became commonplace—even breezy. "How's your sex life?" was the modish greeting to which the expected reply was, "Lousy, how's yours?" Nicholas Courtney, in his study of the Brideshead crowd, *In Society*, reports that the young talked about sex constantly, and with a nonchalance that implied great knowledge. They were, as Evelyn Waugh writes in 1930 in *Vile Bodies*, "sophisticated about sex, before they were at all widely experienced."

In films and fiction, the tremulous virginal heroine gave way to the smoldering vamp, resplendent in feather boa and silk pajamas. In 1926 Elinor Glyn scandalized critics with her best-selling novel *It*. The title, however, was sexier than the book. No longer a neutral pronoun, "It" meant sex appeal as embodied by "It Girl" Clara Bow, America's "Jazz Baby," and the cinema's first sex symbol. Another female icon was Jean Harlow, who in the 1930 film *Hell's Angels* sent shivers down masculine spines when she asked, "Would you be shocked if I put on something more comfortable?"

■ ■ ■

It is the sex instinct which makes women seem beautiful, which they are once in a blue moon, and men seem wise and brave, which they never are at all.

—H. L. MENCKEN,
New York World, September 12, 1926

Two

■ ■ ■

It's a funny thing that people are always quite
ready to admit it if they've no real talent for
drawing or music, whereas everyone imagines
that they themselves are capable of true love,
which is a talent like any other,
only far more rare.

—NANCY MITFORD,
Christmas Pudding, 1976

CYPRIA A woman has not made a conquest until she finds herself pursued [*see* The Conquest *at the end of this chapter*]. Her conquest and the pursuit are synonymous; there cannot be one without the other. And I say that it is desirable for the happiness and well-being of a woman that she should be frequently, or at any rate constantly, pursued—a statement which, as I hope to demonstrate, is not so unprincipled as it sounds.

From innumerable sentimental novels, you will learn the history of a girl who successfully captivates the very first man whom she ever finds attractive—a girl who, though she does everything which in real life would foredoom her chances of conquest, yet utterly enraptures the man of her choice.

Outside the pages of such a volume I have never encountered a woman who could honestly maintain that in her first love affair she achieved a complete victory, or was anything in fact but a dismal failure. So also with men, I believe.

A young person of natural charm and beauty will certainly prove alluring without any definite knowledge of the art of captivation, but to keep alive and warm the desire she has created, she must have a technique—a technique which is usually the result of numerous and varied experiences, but which an intelligent woman might acquire from observation and instruction.

And when I talk of love, do not imagine that I mean any light and transient satisfaction; on the contrary, I wish you to understand the word love in as large a sense as it can hold, as the all-sacrificing, enduring, sympathetic love that is mutual. But true lovers, according to my researches, are the exact reverse of poets, inasmuch as they are made, not born. They have undergone—and not with each other alone—long processes of disappointment, disillusion, pursuit, rebuff, abandon, constraint, and caprice.

In the love affair, as in sculpture, poetry, and every other fine art, no lasting success can be achieved without skill.

You must, of course, have the subjects to practise on. But there is no great difficulty here, since each subject may be made the stepping-stone to another as you grow in skill, until you are expert enough to choose and deserve the ultimate subject beyond whom you will not want to go.[1]

Why did I say that each subject could be made the stepping-stone of another? That must be told, for in telling it I can also make clear why I said it was well for a woman's happiness that she should be pursued—though it should be almost a self-evident proposition by now.

You know that a man does not often want what nobody else would have. He tends rather to covet what others have already found desirable, especially in the way of women. The more proofs he has that you are sought after, the more convinced he will be that you are worth seeking. (Any man

■

[1] *the stepping-stone . . .*
The "stepping-stone theory" coincides with the rise of the modern dating system, which gave women the freedom to sample a variety of men before settling down.

Cypria's offhand dismissal of the rejected "stones" is, like so much during this period, intended to shock. Indeed, she sounds like a character in one of the many postwar drawing-room comedies.

will admit that this is true of any other man, though he will deny it emphatically and sincerely of himself.) Homage begets homage. If you can show, without appearing to flaunt it, that one man has found you worth pursuit, you can very easily awaken the interest of another—granted, of course, certain advantages of propinquity. Should you have developed a little skill from your first experience—which is, after all, the only purpose that trivial experiences have—you can make your second man more eager than the first, and with the second's eagerness you can still more enthral a third. What will have happened to the first man by this time is not my present concern. You may have retained or you may have discarded him, according to your own ends.

Gathering skill and self-confidence and suitors as you proceed, you will have made yourself so irresistible at last that when you discover the man really worthy of permanent attachment, really possible as the companion of a lifetime, you may win him with facility and elegance, and secure him to you for ever without a moment's apprehension. This latter is merely a question of your not letting his love stagnate the moment he has nominally obtained you, but subtly rousing him to fresh pursuit whenever he shows apathy.[2]

See now to what delightful regions your stepping-stones have led you! It only remains for you to learn the knack of making a man happy without surfeiting him, and you will be beloved and protected for the rest of your days.

Is this an evil ambition? No, most decidedly not. Are the means of fulfilling it evil? Let us consider.

■

[2] *This latter is merely a question . . .*
In *Gay Life* (1933), E. M. Delafield presents the Moons, a fashionable couple on holiday. Though married, they are both on the lookout for new partners.

The Moons sat together in silence. The little that they had ever had to say to one another had been said in the course of an electrically-charged fortnight, two years earlier, when they had fallen desperately in love. The rest had been an affair of dancing, drinking, kissing and violent love-making, marriage, and rapid and complete satiety.

■

[3] *The love affair need not be unhappy* . . .

Whatever happened to the dalliance, the fling, the flirtation? Today, three dates constitute a full-fledged "relationship," fraught with "issues" and "agendas." Falling in love at the end of the twentieth century is often accompanied by ardor-dampening discussions of a clinical and hygienic nature. Couples discuss previous intimacies, biological clocks, and the results of medical tests. In the early stages of an affair, nothing can be more alarming than earnestness.

"Haven't you seen how the light touch sometimes, nearly always, in fact, is more effective than the deepest passion?"

"Yes, I have seen that," said Edith, sombre.

"Then, my dear, learn to use it."
—Anita Brookner,
Hotel du Lac, 1986

The love affair handled artistically, as a means to a highly creditable end, is in no sense an immoral practice. I will go further and suggest that so handled it need not be immoral even as an end in itself. Here I know I am treading on delicate ground, and I must go warily. Idealism shrinks from an utterance that sounds so cold-bloodedly cynical, and prudery is naturally horrified. Nevertheless I will tentatively put forward my views, not demanding their acceptance, but merely offering them to your consideration.

The love affair need not be unhappy, deep, and ponderous[3] [*also see* Courtly Love *at the end of this chapter*]. Skilfully handled, it constitutes an art, a delicate and genial art, and one that inspires other arts. It is capable of yielding nothing but delight; or at least there need be no more heartache in it than there is in anything else that is lovely but ephemeral.

A woman with admirers about her will endeavour to be seen at her best at all times: a plain woman will succeed in making herself attractive if she is admired, a pretty woman will grow beautiful. Wit, intellect, talent, even virtue—all reach a higher standard when drawn out by appreciation. And if a higher standard of these best things in life is desirable, you ought not to discountenance any of the ways of bringing it about.

I do not mean, though the pharisaical will pretend to think so, that if everybody indulged in promiscuous flirtation and flattery, the world would be the more agreeable for it. Quite the reverse, for I have hinted before that of all things I most urge discrimination and restraint. An artist, whichever Muse he follow, must be exquisitely selective.

The only justification for an otherwise purposeless love affair lies in its being a work of art and therefore capable of giving pleasure and raising the standard of pleasant things. If it be not a work of art it is worthless, even pernicious, and rather than meddle with it you had better retire to a convent at once.

The Conquest

A woman has not made a conquest . . . (p. 25)
From ancient times, sexual desire and the chase have
been linguistically entwined. "Venery," which means
sexual intercourse or lechery, is a Middle English noun
for the sport of hunting. But it is also descended from
"Venus," "venereal," and "venison," the latter deriving
from the Latin "to hunt." Indeed, the author of a recent
husband-hunting manual provides eighty-five tips to
"Hunters and Huntresses" for capturing their "Quarry."
Today the metaphor of the hunt as lover's pursuit has
assumed a sinister aspect: When a woman is hounded by
an unwelcome male, she is being "stalked."

Images of warfare are more prevalent—and clichéd
—particularly in early love poetry. Elizabethan poet-
asters are slain by cruel mistresses whose eyes are like
killing darts, and so on. Love is perceived in terms of
conquest and surrender, gain or loss. Falling in love is an
act of submission, as if the stricken lover were ceding his
territory, his soul, his very self to the beloved. Con-

versely, when someone inspires love, he or she has made a "conquest." A man's matrimonial conquest is sometimes vulgarly called a "trophy wife," an expression which evokes the unpleasant image of a young bride displayed like a prize kill. In *The Technique*, Cypria seeks to redress the balance of power between the sexes. In this battle, booty is calculated in terms of male admirers.

■ ■ ■

Courtly Love

The love affair need not be unhappy . . . (p. 28)
Can love exist without suffering? Agony is the sine qua non of romance and "rational love" is an oxymoron. Historians tell us that romantic love originated with the troubadours, knights, and poets of eleventh-century France. Men and women had, of course, been falling in and out of love for centuries, but it was then that the conventions of romance in the Western world were codified and called courtly love, with its chivalric code, worship of an unattainable lady, and lover's torment. According to Andreas Cappellaneus, a cleric in the court of Eleanor of Aquitaine and an authority on courtly love, "Love is a

certain inborn suffering derived from the sight of and excessive meditation upon the beauty of the opposite sex, which causes each one to wish above all things the embraces of the other."

Venerated and obeyed, a lady could be surrounded by admirers who were at once her social superiors and her suppliants. On April 24, 1227, in a little town outside Venice, it was announced that the goddess Venus would rise from the sea. The next day a veiled figure, clad in a sumptuous white robe and wearing a headdress of pearls and thick, golden braids, rode into town on a finely caparisoned horse. No one was fooled: Venus's dress hid an unmistakably masculine figure. The Goddess of Love was the knight Ulrich von Lichtenstein, who, braids and robes flying, vanquished every warrior from Venice to Bohemia who challenged him.

For his extraordinary performance, Ulrich was permitted to see and speak to the anonymous princess with whom he had fallen desperately and chastely in love. Perhaps she rewarded him with a kiss. But neither sex nor marriage was the goal of courtly love: Ulrich, in fact, was a married man with three children.

In *The Technique* Moore essentially proposes a twentieth-century version of courtly love: Love is an amusing game in which unapproachable women are hedged in by seemingly insurmountable obstacles, while men experience the tormenting uncertainty of desire. Even married women, Cypria insists, should be surrounded by a coterie of devoted bachelors. Men who fail to observe the niceties of courtship incur their lady's disfavor. And the entire affair, from first glance to final consummation (whatever that may be) is coolly engineered by the woman. Above all, each affair should be conducted with restraint, and according to well-defined rules.

Three

...

For the great majority of mankind are satisfied
with appearances, as though they were
realities and are more often influenced by the
things that seem than by those that are.

—MACHIAVELLI, *Discourses on the
First Ten Books of Titus Livius,* 1513–1517

Love is often nothing but a favorable
exchange between two people who get the most
of what they can expect, considering their value
on the personality market.

—ERICH FROMM, *The Sane Society,* 1955

CYPRIA One of the most painful lessons the virtuous have to learn is that people do not fall in love with virtue.[1] A noble character may enhance the attractions of one already beloved, or it may serve to hold the interest that other charms once awakened, but only in the very rarest instances can it in itself produce the desire for possession.

You choose your friends more deliberately than you choose your lovers, but even in the process of forming friendships virtue is not usually a first consideration. You take to people because they are good company—because they entertain and amuse you, or because they have congenial pursuits, opinions, or moods. The absence of high qualities may afterwards be the reason for *ending* an intimacy, but their presence is not often the reason for beginning one. And if this can be said of those relationships which are at the disposal of common-sense, how much more forcibly does it apply to the emotions which generally insist on being independent of it. If you cannot cultivate any attraction more easily revealed than inward excellence, you will not be besieged with suitors.

This discovery is known to turn good women into bitter ones. Again and again they find themselves, with all their qualities, passed over in favour of others who are merely

■

[1] *One of the most painful lessons . . .*
  That virtue alone will never quicken a man's love subverts almost everything girls are taught about finding True Love. Fairy tales, classic novels, and pop fiction all tell their readers that good girls triumph, particularly if they suffer—and preferably in silence.

  In contrast, *The Technique* presents the *Realpolitik* of romance, in which allure triumphs over morality. Despite the frivolous nature of her subject, Moore's precepts are supported by two great unbiased observers of nature, both human and animal: Darwin and Machiavelli.

  In the natural world, Darwin tells us, it is the gaudy, the strong, and the wily that prevail. In politics, according to Machiavelli, honor and rectitude are meaningless; power and victory belong to the cunning ruler who manipulates his subjects while preserving the appearance of virtue.

  Modern men, Cypria insists, are

equally susceptible to the trappings of beauty, rank, and wealth. Her tactics, like those of Machiavelli, are motivated by hard, practical concerns, not moral or idealistic ones. But she is not as ruthless or as unprincipled as Machiavelli: Decency is good policy and moral integrity need not impede one's technique. Bad behavior is, as her countrymen would say, "unsporting."

■

2 There is one factor without which . . .

The word "prestige" comes from the French *prestige*, "illusion," and the Latin *praestigiae*, "tricks." Anything that invests a woman with allure while making her appear somewhat unattainable creates prestige, which, in this instance, is almost synonymous with sexual power.

pretty, vivacious, or clever, until they grow to regard beauty, and vivacity, and so forth with that antagonism which only jealousy engenders. It would not have been thus if they had realised early in youth that in order to be sought after they must develop some sprightlier allurement than virtue.

"But," you may say, "what of the women who have no possibility of developing allurements?"

They are unfortunate indeed, but there are not so many of them as you might think. Almost every woman has something about her which, carefully nurtured, will make her seem desirable—not, of course, to every man in her world, but to one or two. The charm, which may be anything from piquant conversation to good cooking, will find appreciation somewhere if it be well displayed. But it is obvious that a woman endowed with assets of all kinds needs less dexterity in order to be captivating than one who must depend on a meagre few. You must, in other words, proportion your dexterity to your eligibility, and for this it behooves you to know exactly how eligible you are. I will therefore devote this chapter to the consideration of assets.

There is one factor without which no woman can have any power over men; and which is consequently so vital that it must be printed in italics.[2] It is *prestige*. Prestige may grow from a variety of causes, and may exist in any quantity or quality. There are numerous ways of acquiring it, and numerous ways of losing it; but the one certain way of flinging it to the winds is to let any man with whom you may concern yourself become aware that he is more significant to you than you are to him, and the one certain way of building it up is to be, or at least seem, spiritually independent of him. Prestige will increase your value in the eyes of even the least impressionable men, and you may use it to give you the enchanting air of being unattainable.

Webster defines prestige as "weight or influence derived from past success; force or charm derived from acknowledged character or reputation." With this definition in view, let me place the prestigious attractions in order, not of merit, but of puissance.

- Beauty
- Fame
- Wealth
- Rank
- Social popularity
- Intellect
- Domestic and other special talents exerted privately

If you are romantic you will be disgusted to find Wealth and Rank placed before Intellect, and Virtue nowhere at all, but I ask you to set aside sentimental prejudice as far as you possibly can while I expound. You would like to believe, I dare say, that a woman who is simply good has just as much chance of attaching an admirer as one who is simply rich or simply famous, but it won't do. Men are appealed to through their vanity and vainglory even more easily than women, which means that most men would rather be seen about with a woman who patently did credit to their own powers of fascination, than with the worthiest creature in the world if she had no means of making the beholders envy them.

I think I hear you exclaim: "Men may like to be *seen about* with the most obviously attractive women, irrespective of their characters, but when it comes to making a permanent choice . . ."

Ah, my dear Saccharissa, discard that old-fashioned idea, preached by dreary elders for their own ends, and countless times disproven. Men want to marry the sort of women they like to be seen about with. To say otherwise is to fly in the face of evidence. In fact "wanting to marry" is often a synonym for "wanting to be seen about with," and innumerable unions are based on nothing firmer than that.

And of those attributes of woman which most satisfy man's pride, or vanity, none is more potent than Beauty [*see* Sex Appeal *at the end of this chapter*]. By being of all allurements the easiest to bring to the notice of every man, it produces prestige the most rapidly, and is therefore far and away the most valuable—extrinsically at least. The successes throughout history of women with nothing but Beauty and a due complement of discrimination to aid them are so notable as to make any elaboration here unnecessary.

Next I fancy man's chief weakness is for Fame, because, like Beauty, it reflects its glory upon him. It is capable indeed of shedding even more glamour, but Beauty—besides its sensual appeal—has one advantage; namely, that it can be recognised instantaneously and admired anywhere in the world, whereas Fame is not effective outside its own sphere. A dancer of renown in Madrid, for instance, might pass for a nonentity in London, and vice versa, but a lovely woman has a universal influence. Moreover, she is just as likely to delight a great man as a humble one, while Fame is not often in itself an attraction except to the unimportant.

Yet Fame is a powerful asset, since she who possesses it will be so sought after as to appear at times inaccessible, and nothing arouses the instinct of the hunter so rapidly as what seems difficult to obtain. It is the glamour of Fame which lends to actresses three parts of their notable fascination.

And the reason why an eminent actress receives so many more masculine attentions than—say—an equally eminent and agreeable sculptress or painter is, of course, because, her person as well as her name being known to the world, a man may be fairly sure of creating an impression with her anywhere inside a certain environment, whereas the other's identity must be made known before he can be duly credited with a reputable conquest.

All this, you think, accords ill with the common notion that men prefer not to make love to women who outshine them; yet it is true—and the common notion is also true. Men undoubtedly do not like to be eclipsed by women, but the fact that a woman has a greater reputation than her associates need not at all imply that she eclipses them. On the contrary, they who might otherwise have lived and died unnoticed will probably obtain some degree of distinction in the eyes of the world only because she has singled them out for favour. Far from being eclipsed, they shine the brighter for her radiance.

But I don't want you to imagine, dearest creature, that I class the greater part of mankind as a vast horde of tuft-

■

³ *The object appearing* nearly *unattainable* . . .

The qualifier "nearly" is crucial. Researchers corroborate what lovers instinctively know: Hope and despair are the linchpins of desire. In highly charged romances, the partner who loves the most careens from one pole to the other. Uncertainty, as Oscar Wilde observed, is the essence of romantic love.

hunters blatantly running after people whose acquaintance they can boast about. The average man does not consciously reflect: "This woman is in the public eye, and if I can get her to go about with me, her presence will attract respectful attention towards myself. Therefore I will pursue her." Rather, he is impressed by her position almost in spite of himself. He really believes he is surveying the famous, or wealthy, or nobly-born personage impartially, and all the time his eyes are dazzled by the glitter of her consequence. The object appearing *nearly* unattainable,[3] appears also desirable (note that *total* unattainability is no attraction); desire urges pursuit; pursuit lasts until hope is worn out or the goal completely won.

After Fame I placed Wealth as most productive of prestige. Wealth means *background*. The rich woman can not only make herself seem aloof—and the value of aloofness has been fully emphasised—but she can "stage" herself in the manner best calculated to heighten her charms and suppress her defects. Few people of either sex, and then only rather dull ones, ever thoroughly outgrow the child's love of the spectacular. Jewels, clothes, perfumes, exotic flowers, splendid rooms, French maids, flunkeys—we laugh at such panoply in novels and films, but in real life it has a power which can subdue even conscience and common-sense. Besides, with money a woman has at her disposal every aid and accessory to Beauty, and she must be particularly plain or singularly lacking in taste and invention if she cannot buy for herself some claim, however fragile, to good looks (*see* Buying Beauty *at the end of this chapter*). Think what can be done by means of dress alone, and how fine the dimmest gem will look if only the setting is superb enough!

Rank is one degree less in importance. (Under this heading I wish to include all the kinds of social eminence that are not due either to public distinction or to sheer personal popularity.) If I were discussing the attitude of women to men, instead of the reverse, I should place Rank before Wealth, for women seem to be more readily swayed by it— not without reason, since men may confer their rank upon their wives, and women cannot do the same by their husbands. Rank *per se* does not captivate the normal modern man, but it is a good asset, because, generally speaking, it still causes those who have it to be hedged about with barriers, and still provides an excellent background. A man may quite genuinely profess indifference to noble lineage and high position and yet be influenced all unaware by the poise and circumstances of the person endowed with them. And there is the satisfaction of reflected glory. Although *he* may not care about inherited honours and other arbitrary distinctions, he must be conscious of the fact that many other people do, and that he exalts himself in the estimation of his acquaintance by being in favour with the elect.

This must naturally be understood to apply only to a man who has no direct claim to social notability, for it is obvious that he who himself occupies a high station is immune from all the considerations to which I have referred. The barriers would not exist for him, and would therefore perform no tantalising and seductive function; the background might still evoke respect, but would have no novelty to excite attention and wonder; and he would have nothing to gain by being known to consort with the women of his own world. He could, without doubt, arouse more interest by doing the opposite.

And indeed it is to be noted of Fame and Wealth, as well as of Rank—all attractions, in short, that make their appeal to instincts coarse and tawdry—that they are efficacious chiefly upon those who do not possess them. The nonentity courts the celebrity, the impecunious are unconsciously entranced by the splendour and freedom of the rich, and the humble are glad to be satellites to the lofty. But the appeal of Beauty, Intellect, and Character is not to coarse instincts, and here there is no reason why like should not attract like. A handsome man will be just as liable as a plain one to fall in love with a woman for her Beauty alone, whereas if a famous man falls in love with a famous woman, it is not because of her renown but through something else about her, and he would be equally enamoured were she obscure.

Somewhat less potent than Rank is the prestige it creates, although you might well expect it to be more so, is the kind of social eminence which proceeds not from accident of birth or fortune, but from agreeableness of personality. By having adaptable, pleasing, and genial manners, a ready sympathy, or a compelling wit, a person not otherwise favoured by Providence may achieve such a popularity in his or her particular circle as to be constantly sought after, and by being sought after may gradually acquire that air of importance which so enhances one human being's value in the eyes of another.

You might wonder why personality should not prove more engaging than most of the assets already described, and so it would be if snobbery were a less prevalent foible.

But whereas personality is not prestigious until it has come to be recognised and acknowledged, those other assets carry a prestige in themselves, and automatically make the possessor seem difficult of approach. A striking character is not necessarily remote, and generally requires external assistance in order to become so. Many a woman of vivid personality is so easy of access as to be held rather in contempt than in demand.

As to Intellect, when it is unaccompanied by Fame or Popularity it is more likely to prove a liability than an asset as far as the majority of men are concerned; but since for a certain rare few it is the mightiest of all attractions, it has its place in my list.[4] The average man decidedly shrinks from what he calls a "brainy" or "highbrow" woman, and if she is in the unfortunate position of having to secure his attention, no man of her own type being available, she must conceal her intellectuality instead of trying to use it as a blandishment, which is a mistake very frequently made. Not until Intellect has acquired either social or public distinction does it intrigue the ordinary mind, and even then it is the result, not the cause, which awakens admiration. When it meets with a kindred spirit, however, it can achieve a conquest both quick and sure.

Lastly, we come to what I have termed "domestic and other special talents exerted privately"—good housewifery, skill in games, musical ability, and so forth. Though one of these, unless developed to an extraordinary degree, will not be enough by itself to make a woman much sought after, in propitious circumstances it will render her desirable. A man fond of music, for example, but with few opportunities of

■

[4] *As to Intellect . . .*
Until World War I, women's intellectual inferiority to men was "an established fact," confirmed by both the Bible and science (the male brain's larger size was deemed proof of his intellectual supremacy).

In countless movies, plays, and novels, the intellectual female is a no-nonsense, no-frills career woman, high-strung, plain, and repressed. She might be the heroine's wise-cracking best friend or the heroine herself—a spectacled, uptight spinster who, much to her surprise, discovers her susceptibility to masculine charms. In the denouement she removes her spectacles (the badge of the undesirable), her resistance crumbles, and a voluptuous "real" woman emerges.

Since qualities such as intelligence and virtue are not exclusive to either sex, they are not usually regarded as attractive to men. A student in graduate school, lamenting that her lover had left her for one of his students in English 101, wailed, "And she doesn't even know how to use a comma!" Usually, the more feminine the woman, the greater her chances for success in the evolutionary struggle.

College women in general found it more difficult to marry:
Men still want wives who will bolster their egos rather than detract from them. —Paul H. Landis, *Your Marriage and Family Living*, 1954

hearing it, may be so delighted with the playing of even a moderate performer that he will long for greater and greater intimacy with the being who can give him so much pleasure, and in that intimacy he may possibly find what will inspire affection. Such an asset must be used carefully by a woman who has no other. It is her last resource, and she should cultivate it to the utmost.

But it is unlikely that any one of the advantages I have tabulated will be your only possession. The majority of women are not heavily endowed with any single advantage or virtue, but have a little of two or three—a little Beauty, say, a little Popularity, and a little Intellect; or some share of Wealth with a modest supply of Beauty and Talent.

And here I will break off and give you leisure to take stock of your own assets. However excellent they may be, they will not create love, but they are the snares which trap attention and interest, and the mainsprings of the desire for possession. The growth of deeper feeling will depend upon your qualities and your skill.

Sex Appeal

And of those attributes . . . (p. 40)

Whether it takes the form of the baboon's puffy red buttocks or the demimonde's shocking red lips, beauty, the sensory appreciation of the "Other," is a sexual magnet. The apprehension of beauty is an emotional as well as physical experience. An unexpected gesture, a slight turn of the neck, can suddenly transform a plain woman into a lovely one. Conversely, a lovely woman can say something ugly, and turn herself into a fishwife. Yet a sexy young woman is the ultimate trophy. Older women may complain, but there's a reason why youth is associated with beauty: Fertility peaks when a woman looks her best (another of nature's tricks to promote the survival of the species).

Americans (both men and women) worship beauty to the exclusion of every other feminine attribute, and they favor blond, blue-eyed women with large breasts and big lips. After World War II, when sales of beauty products boomed, plainness was regarded as a serious offense.

The author of a 1946 husband-hunting manual advises the homely: "Since a feeling of confidence and poise is so important in winning a mate it might be advisable for one with a bad nose, for example, to have a plastic surgery. . . ." Another warns: "If you are not gifted with a perfect figure and flawless skin, there is only one solution for you. You must apply yourself relentlessly to the task of making nature over so that you can take your place without self-consciousness in the race for a husband." Self-assurance and poise are thus important, but they can, according to these manuals, only be achieved through an exacting regimen of dieting, surgery, and beauty preparations.

In a 1962 article in *Esquire,* Robert Benton and Gloria Steinem dispense Machiavellian advice for the would-be campus prince: "If your date is very good-looking, exploit it. Meet her at your dorm and take her to college places. If your date is not very good-looking, tell your friends you are having an affair with a married woman and take her to the movies." As Beth Bailey wryly notes in *From Front Porch to Back Seat* (1988), "Better to be known as an adulterer than a man who goes out with a homely woman."

A good-looking woman makes a man look good: In *A Natural History of the Senses* (1990), Diane Ackerman cites a study in which people examined photographs of a couple and evaluated only the man. If the woman with him was attractive, he was perceived as smarter and more successful than if the woman was plain.

Of course, sex appeal is more than just good looks. The French term *jolie laide* refers to a seeming contradiction: the unattractive woman whose very homeliness gives her a strange allure. History is filled with women who, while not conventionally beautiful, possessed an indefinable quality that made them irresistible to men. Intelligent and seductive, they transcended the social and sexual conventions of their age: Madame de Staël, George Sand, Alma Mahler, to cite a few. These women attract men of wealth, genius, and power; in other words, men who can resist the pressure to be like everyone else. The majority of men, as Cypria points out, tend to be conformists, preferring women who look and act like their peers—only better.

Obviously physically unattractive women are loved, sometimes by handsome men. One doesn't need beauty, per se, just the prestige it imparts and the resulting self-confidence. A beautiful woman will almost always attract men, but appearance alone is only the lure, not the hook.

■ ■ ■

Buying Beauty

Besides, with money . . . (p. 42)

Beauty treatments and accessories have long been viewed as the province of the idle rich. An 1892 manual, *My Lady's Dressing Room,* refers to nonsurgical rhinoplasty, an expensive procedure in which a corrective device is applied to the offending nose. The author approvingly remarks that the famous beauty Lady Londonderry preserved her complexion by spending every tenth day in bed. The rich could also visit spas and patronize innovative couturiers like Chanel, Poiret, and Schiaparelli.

Before 1914, women concocted homemade beauty treatments consisting of such ingredients as vinegar, oatmeal, rosewater, borax, and lemon. By 1920, they could buy inexpensive ready-made products; makeup, from kohl to lip rouge, was readily available. Shop clerks could look like society ladies now that mass-produced clothing resembled haute couture, and the advent of the permanent wave allowed any woman to toss girlish curls. Few, however, could have foreseen that the disfigurements of war would give rise to a medical specialty that would become known as cosmetic surgery.

Four

■ ■ ■

. . . And as to intense *passion,* I am convinced
that it is no desirable feeling. In the first place,
it seldom or never meets with a requital,
and, in the second place, if it did, the feeling
would be only temporary: it would last the
honeymoon, and then, perhaps, give place to
disgust or indifference. . . . Certainly this would
be the case on the man's part; and on the
woman's—God help her if she is left to love
passionately and alone.

—CHARLOTTE BRONTË, in a letter

CYPRIA   The various emotions, Saccharissa, which I endeavour to treat of in these pages have little to do with Love—Love with a capital letter as poets and novelists set it down, Love eternal, immutable, incorruptible. Love that cannot possibly come more than once into any life; in short, the Love that nearly all of us at some time in our youth have imagined we were feeling.

If such Love exists it is obviously out of place in this account of the Technique of the Love Affair, for the plain reason that so sublime a sensation could no more need a technique in the handling than the music of the angels.

True, it is difficult to prove that these "twin souls," for whom there are no doubts, no hesitations, no caprices, have any entity outside the romancer's invention, the young lover's fancy, and the mind of the occultist. I will not irritate your romantic sensibility by any futile attempt at disillusion: but I must at once explain that although the notion of celestial Love may strain my own credulity, I do not scoff at the earthy but still beautiful emotion called love.

That overworked word may be found with a quite separate kind of value in the phrase "*in* love," "I love you," and "I am in love with you," [1] are expressions which have, as

■

[1] *That overworked word may . . .*
After studying the behavior of people "in love," the psychologist Dorothy Tennov coined the word "limerance" to describe the rich panoply of feelings and sensations—tremors, palpitations, exhilaration, and despair—that we ascribe to the condition "being in love."

■

²*Infatuation is blind* . . .

Historically more distant case studies of obsession seem less the stuff of tabloids than legends, their pathology a reflection of the lover's capacity for deep feeling. Adèle Hugo, the daughter of Victor Hugo and the subject of a 1975 film by François Truffaut, is a textbook illustration of love *in extremis*. Driven by her passion for a caddish soldier, Adèle follows him from France to Nova Scotia and suffers a breakdown from which she never recovers.

"Oh, God, give me the Duke of Hamilton and I will make him happy," wrote fourteen-year-old Marie Bashkirtseff about a man she had never met. For the next year, she charts the vicissitudes of her one-sided romance, filling dozens of notebooks with her outpourings. Her entire diary, which fills 104 notebooks and ends with her death in 1884, provides an unnerving look inside the claustrophobic world of the obsessive lover.

you well know, two different meanings, though they are often confounded. We regard love as the highest and most selfless feeling of which human beings are capable, but "being in love" is a sensation which is essentially founded on an acute desire for possession, or, in happy cases, a deep satisfaction in possession.

The sources of the possessive desire between man and woman may be placed roughly in four categories: namely, physical attraction, affection, admiration, and self-interest. Self-interest must be understood to mean merely the study of one's own convenience in a mundane sense—the motive, for instance, which actuates fortune-hunters in preparing for marriage—and as it can claim no kinship of any sort with love, nothing more need be said of it in the present chapter.

Now let us see what kinship with love can be boasted by the other agents. First we will take affection, the warm and tender regard one entertains for one's familiar friends. This *is* love, a mild and less enduring variety of it; love, as the French proverb says, with his wings—and, I may add, not without his eyes. Infatuation is blind,² admiration is all eyes, affection alone has normal vision. It is clearly not to be very rapidly aroused; furthermore, the possessive tendency which it induces will only become urgent and irresistible under specially favourable conditions, such as loneliness on the one side, or a great need of protection on the other. But there is another sort of affection—that which not infrequently follows upon physical attraction or admiration, and may ultimately appear in the large and comprehensive form of love.

Physical attraction itself, when it is unaccompanied by affection, appears in but two forms. Either it is recognised without delusions by the person who feels it, in which event it is described as lust; or else, especially from prudery or innocence, it is disguised in the mind as some other emotion, generally love itself, and becomes in a greater or less degree infatuation.

This curious and interesting state of mind has usually all the symptoms of that Love (observe the capital) with which I do not concern myself, except one alone: *it is very rarely mutual.* It is common to the unsophisticated, the repressed, the idealistic, all those, in fact, who cannot or will not recognise a deep fleshly instinct when they meet it, and who—to borrow a word from the new psychology[3]—inwardly "sublimate"[4] it until it assumes a dangerously romantic aspect. Others who succumb to infatuation are those who, through lack of confidence in themselves and fear of failure, gradually place a higher and higher value on what seems so hard to attain, or so difficult to keep, until at last they lose all sense of proportion.

The ambition of people who are "madly in love"[5]—a description which is here perfectly applicable—is a complete and triumphant possession of the desired object, and they almost invariably defeat their own ends at every point. On the very rare occasions when this passion does achieve its purpose, it is satiated and subsides, giving place to affection or indifference, but more often still to a reactionary dislike. In general, however, owing to the follies engendered by excessive emotion, an infatuated person comes nowhere near to complete possession.

■

[3] *. . . the new psychology . . .*

Psychoanalysis, specifically the work of Sigmund Freud.

■

[4] *. . . "sublimate" . . .*

By the 1920s, Freudian jargon such as "libido," "id," and "super-ego" had entered mass culture. While the average person had only a vague sense of their meaning, everyone understood that the terms had something to do with sex. The sexually deprived were airily advised to "sublimate," much as they might be told to take up clog dancing. By World War II, the term sublimation had assumed an immediacy for women faced with a shortage of men. One Englishwoman who had lost her fiancé asked the "agony aunt" at *Women's Own* magazine: "My friend says that spinsters should learn to sublimate. What does this mean?"

■

[5] *The ambition of people "madly in love" . . .*

Love as lunacy is not just a poetic conceit. Indeed, what is taken for love can veer dangerously toward mental illness. Consider three modern and much-talked-about cases: A judge stalks and threatens the lover who jilted him; the headmistress of a prestigious boarding school shoots and kills the man who scorned her; a biologist murders a prostitute with whom he is obsessed. All these offenders were once considered "normal," and all believed themselves in love.

■

⁶*Everything connected with him* . . .
    When Dorothy Tennov studied the "mating" behavior of students at the University of Bridgeport, she observed that they tended to focus on certain features of the beloved. This process, which she called "crystallization," differs from idealization. All of Tennov's subjects could easily list their loved one's defects, yet they either dismissed them or found them endearing. (After the enchantment fades, it's precisely those endearing traits that irritate the lover, eventually driving him or her away.)

She—I presume for the sake of consistency a being of our own sex—she longs to make the man in question love her; or rather, to put it more accurately, she longs to make him share all her own extravagant sensations which she believes to be love. This would be easy enough if she had her wits about her, and could proceed with deliberation and artifice; but as it is, her armoury is locked, her weapons are left to rust, and she is furnished with nothing.

She translates his animal appeal for her into the highest realms of romantic passion, and perceives him as enveloped in glamour. Everything connected with him acquires by degrees a kind of enchantment for her, his very faults having a perverted charm.⁶ The casual mention of his name will cause her heart to beat faster, she thinks of him incessantly, and is wistfully jealous of everything that occupies him; his work, his masculine pleasures, his friends and relations, all are at once hallowed and hateful.

I have said that the most certain way of losing prestige is to let a man see that he occupies a more important place in your mind than you in his, but a woman who is infatuated will find it difficult, however circumspect she may be, to conceal her feelings. It is more than likely that in some wild moment she will openly avow them. Whether this be so or not, he is almost certain to realise somehow or other that he has made a conquest, and unless she were to fall out of love with him completely on that instant, she has lost him. Good or bad, merciful or ruthless, all human creatures are the same in this—the knowledge that there is a soul desperate with devotion before them can only excite pity or amusement, exactly as if they saw the other grovelling not in the spirit but in the flesh.

If this man were heartless enough to be amused and show it, he would unwittingly be doing her a kindness, for then she might sooner be brought back to her senses; but to spare her pain, he will probably pretend to more than he feels. Thus he will merely prolong and not lessen her misery. Forced embraces and protests of love that spring only from habit or good-nature must always lack conviction, and though she may try to delude herself, she is aware that she is as far from complete possession as if she had never met him.

In her abjectness and anxiety she ceases even to be congenial company for the man to whom she longs to appear beautiful and elusive. Her unhappiness is simply tedious, and he begins to chafe under his responsibility. "Do you love me?" she demands, and his jaded reply, "Of course," should warn her from ever asking again, but it does not.

The day comes when he can sustain the pose no longer. Perhaps he has been honest enough never to enter into it quite fully, perhaps, almost in spite of himself, he has always refrained from the finite word that would have committed him. And now some incident, some special tax upon his honour or his independence, brings him to the climax. He tells her frankly that his "love" is over, or that it never existed.

At first, all delight seems to be extracted from her life, and the world tastes bitter with humiliation and defeat. False pride says, "Kill yourself!" Folly says, "Win him back!" False pride has been known to prevail, Folly gains attention often, common-sense rarely. If she embark upon the usual pathetic endeavour to win him back, whatever form it takes—a series of proofs of her devotion, a new display of fascinations, an appeal to his gratitude or his integrity, according to what her relations with him may have been—whatever form it takes, it is foredoomed. She must admit her failure, and retire to dismal solitude, or throw herself upon the sympathy of her friends. Her grief will be long in proportion to the intensity with which she has felt. Long or short, she believes it will last for ever, that she will never love anyone else, and never enjoy anything else while she lives.

But gradually the malady of mind is dispersed; fresh interests seduce her attention, and at last she finds that she can hear his name without a pang, except for the fatuity of her own behaviour. She sees him as he is, and there is a considerable chance that in the future she will vigorously deny that she ever cared a jot for him, and believe it too.

Such is the common end of a common case of infatuation, but, as I have hinted, there is also another kind of awakenment, and a far pleasanter one. The man, even when stripped of his glamour, may prove to be still charming and worthy of respect. In this happy event, the woman, while discarding her previous false valuation, will accept the friendship he has doubtless offered in lieu of love, or will herself make candid overtures of friendship.

There have been infatuations that were never cured,[7] and which have consequently been regarded as revelations of true Love, but you will notice that the sufferers were always of three types: those whose youth was ended, and who felt powerless either to replace the lost lover or to develop new interests; those who retired to monasteries, convents, and other isolated places, for the express purpose of treasuring up their misery and whose solitary and unnatural lives made healthy recovery impossible; and those deprived of the object of their passion not by wholesome disillusionment, but through death, or some other circumstance more likely to shed glamour than to destroy it.

Infatuation is a wildly exaggerated and undiscriminating kind of admiration, which sometimes springs up as an excuse for a craving of the body. Admiration, however, may also exist without any noticeable physical attraction, and still produce—in a far less hectic degree—the desire for possession. A man, for instance, may quite calmly and distantly admire a woman's beauty, intelligence, or talent. He would be willing to go on approving calmly and distantly for ever, were his vanity not aroused by seeing others pursue her, and he seeks to gain possession of her merely for the triumph of obtaining what many others want. He convinces himself that he loves the woman, and perhaps in the end he really will love her. That will depend on her.

Many marriages are the result of admiration rationalised into love. The triumph of getting what other people want, or seem to want, is only complete when one can show the other people that one has got it. Of course, only hardened cynics would marry with the full and frank knowledge that they were actuated by piqued vanity alone. Most admirers

■

[7] *There have been infatuations that were never cured . . .*

The love potion that induces the madness of infatuation is known as PEA, or phenylethylamine. One glance—and it usually *is* a glance—from the right person releases a spurt of PEA, a chemical that accelerates the transmission of information from one nerve cell to the next. It's a high-octane rush of desire, hope, and energy in which one is quite literally "turned on." It's the surge of PEA that makes love initially so exhilarating and enables lovers to stay up for hours just thinking about one another.

One man-hunting guide guarantees that any woman can get any man to fall in love with her by stimulating his production of PEA. The author offers eighty-five techniques that will accomplish this end. One question: Is the man really in love or does he just feel as if he is?

---

believe that they are lovers too when they begin pursuit, and after the turmoil of attainment, affection and love itself frequently ensue.

Infatuation rarely concludes in permanent union because of its habit of defeating its own end. Admiration, which is so much more wary, often finds the means of being requited.

Five

■ ■ ■

Romantic obsession is by its nature
self-consuming. It never ends in stable love,
except perhaps by extraordinary accident.

—ROBERT KAREN, psychologist
Elle, 1997

CYPRIA A successful love affair is one which results either in permanent mating or in mutual friendship, and for this nothing is more efficacious than to inspire in your subject an admiration kept so perpetually alert that it almost reaches the high pitch of infatuation, but does not quite. Extravagant emotions should be avoided, although—and this is significant!—you are not secure unless you know that you *could* make him feel extravagantly if it were necessary. And you should have control over your own emotions as well as his, for remember, if he should once see that you have given him a more important place in life than he has given you, you have lost your prestige, which is almost a synonym for your power. If he does occupy this superior position, you can, by using every art of which you are capable, prevent his being aware if it, but it is a tedious business, and it is better if possible to check your ardour before it reaches the stage at which it needs to be concealed. You may feel whatever you please so long as it does not reach the infatuation point; he, as I have said, should be kept near that point, but should not be driven beyond it unless his conduct be such as to merit that sort of punishment.

How can you keep your ardour in check? That question

strikes to the very root of half the "love" problems ever mooted. If you could always feel just as keenly as was necessary for the enjoyment of the situation and could repress all superfluous emotion with ease, how simply and triumphantly you might conduct your affairs! The one thing essential is self-confidence, for the fear of not being able to retain your admirer, or to replace him if you lost him, is pretty certain sooner or later to lend him an importance in your thoughts quite disproportionate to his merits. But if you are unwaveringly sure of yourself, and are free from all the alarms of a woman troubled with a sense of inferiority, your judgment will be cool and clear, and, in short, you *cannot* become infatuated.

In attaining this serenity nothing succeeds like success. When you can look back upon a series of victories, you will probably be immune from anxiety as to the issue of any new foray. However, everyone must make a beginning, and in case you have not yet reached the stage where you can gain strength from the memory of former conquests—in case you are even, perhaps, hampered by the recollection of failure—I will give you some counsel.

In the first place, when you find yourself standing on the threshold of a love affair, take care that you do not turn your back upon old friends and interests in a manner you will afterwards regret. Never will they be more useful to you than now, when you will need all the diversions at your command to prevent your mind from fixing too firmly on one object. Remember also that as often as your lover, or prospective lover, sees you engrossed with people and things to the apparent exclusion of himself, he will be stimulated to a fresh effort to win you. And should the affair eventually fall through, how much lighter will be your pangs if it is only one attachment severed among many that remain. You will probably have a strong temptation to forsake your usual interests, and to yield yourself up utterly to the pleasures (and undoubtedly, in such an event, the pains) of your enamoured state; but resist it, my dear friend, with all your vitality, and each time you do so the task will become easier.

The women who make the abysmal error of discarding any admirer or admirers they may already have, are stripping themselves of the glamour which the state of being desired by others would lend them in the eyes of the man they want. And by giving him no reason for vigilance, they soon give him every reason for indifference. And when he grows indifferent, can they find "flattering unction" in the continued homage of another wooer? No, dearest Saccharissa, they are stranded.

If only they would not make a virtue of their folly! They tell you: "I was so faithful to him. I gave up everyone for him." Well, is this not enough to surfeit any man?

This quixotic sort of mismanagement reminds me of the next portion of the advice I have for you. Do not, I beg, permit yourself the luxury of *thinking romantically*. Reject all hackneyed and meaningless "ideals." They make a fool of you. I have known women who refused to countenance any artificial means of winning devotion, who imagined that "love would beget love," and that if they emptied the vials of their affection upon a man, he would surely do the same by them. Such a delusion can create nothing but mis-

■

[1] *These first and last affairs are generally* . . .

The novelist Susan Hill observes that the middle-aged love affair is the most anguished of them all. Perhaps this is because mature lovers can appreciate love while recognizing its transience.

ery. It is one which we nearly all harbour at the beginning and at the end of our amatory careers—at the beginning, because adolescence is unreasonably optimistic; at the end, because in the last desperate encounter with passion we grow frantic in the terror of failure and, losing our heads, fling away all the weapons of experience.

These first and last affairs are generally the unhappiest of our lives,[1] and the mistakes which pervade them take root, more often than not, in an ill-judged romanticism. The high-flown notion of self-abnegation, for instance—of devoting your whole being to your love at any cost—will make the best-natured man grow restive, if it is put into practice.

Then, again, many romantic-minded women have deplorably misleading ideas centering on—O baneful word! —"soul-mates." They conceive that for every woman one man has been specially created by a benign Providence, and when they fall in love they very naturally imagine that they have met that Man. The preposterous blundering to which such a belief must lead need hardly be described. The craftsmanship by which they really could attach the lover permanently is ignored; and when, as the result of their own ineptitude, he falls away from them, they suffer appallingly because they have convinced themselves that no other man in the whole world will ever be able to content them. It is certainly true that most human beings, even those who do not believe in "soul-mates," are prone to over-value the object they have lost, but not to the extent of these idealistic women.

But none of the follies that spring from a false idealism is so harmful in its effects as the habit of investing quite drab and ordinary incidents with an atmosphere that makes them appear rich and strange. In eyes which see things thus, a trivial flirtation becomes the chase of Daphne and Apollo, a physical union based on mere lust seems like the marriage of Cupid and Psyche, a common jilting produces the Anguish of Œnone deserted by Paris.[2] In this manner many a woman (and man too, though that is not to my purpose) is bereft of all discrimination.

To a young creature whose head is full of fantasies, some sordid little intrigue with a cad may take on the aspect of an amour with a god, but her exalted attitude of mind will not prevent the consequences that are likely to ensue.

You might at first believe that an idealist would be more selective than a prosaic thinker, that none save those who came up to her extravagantly high standard would find favour with her, yet this is far from being the case. Physical attraction must play its part in her life, and it is no respecter of standards; but whereas the practical woman will be awake to the real nature of her feelings, the idealist unconsciously disguises them until they appear as nothing less than Love (capital Love).[3] The practical woman is the more selective of the two, since she will not allow herself to be agreeably blinded to disagreeable realities, and is therefore not likely to be fascinated long by a worthless philanderer, or to yield much to him. And if she has not the ecstasy of thinking she is wooed by a divinity, neither does she taste the irony of finding out that all her idyllics and heroics have been, at the best, merely comical.

Another precept for the preservation of your dignity

■

[2] *Daphne and Apollo, Cupid and Psyche, Œnone and Paris . . .*
These couples from classical mythology are the embodiment of desire *in extremis.*

■

[3] *. . . the idealist unconsciously disguises them until . . .*
Unable to accept or acknowledge her "animal instincts," a naive woman might mistake a one-night stand for a romantic tryst. Cheap romance novels exploit this tendency, transforming sex into an act of choreographed abandonment in an exotic and/or historical setting. The hero may be violent, ruthless, or hungry, but readers never forget that he's in love and will soon be married. All devotees of romance fiction know that seminudity, heaving breasts, hungry lips, and burning kisses are signs of true love between "soul mates."

arises out of this warning: Be very careful how you write ardent love-letters, even to a man from whom you receive them [*see* On the Love Letter *at the end of this chapter*]. Such correspondence, having been put away as a cherished treasure, has an unhappy knack of coming to light and being re-read after a love affair has expired. Phrases of soulful yearning and extravagant devotion must be heard only in a propitious atmosphere, otherwise they will be ludicrous or pathetic.

If you can write exquisitely, however, and are addressing yourself to one who can appreciate your composition in an

abstract manner, there is no reason why you should hide your light under a bushel. He cannot laugh at a letter whose literary quality he esteems—provided, of course, that the emotions it expresses are not beyond the bounds of reason. But so few men are æsthetic in these matters, that for general purposes you should make no attempt to write beautiful things to a lover. Yet in order not to sound unattractively frigid or indifferent when you communicate with him from a distance, you must manage to convey some warmth, and amorous warmth too if you have reached a pass where that is not indiscreet.

The best way of doing this is lightly and playfully. A gay, teasing letter, only half-serious, will not look so absurd, after the almost inevitable termination of your amour, as vows of eternal fidelity.

You might think that he should desist from writing very zealously to you for the same reason, but such things do not

work both ways, dear Saccharissa. Love-letters are the trophies of your skill, and from occasionally surveying them,
even when they touch your sentiment no longer, you may
gain confidence and strength for further victories. But men
are never, in modern times, expected to have trophies of
their amatory conquests, neither do they dwell upon former
triumphs for the sake of self-encouragement. Their natural
confidence and strength, aided by our social codes, are
already so considerable that they have little need of your
generosity in upholding them. They, on the other hand, can
well afford to treat you handsomely, and it is nothing less
than your moral duty to make sure that they do so.

On the Love Letter

Be very careful how you write ardent love-letters . . . (p. 70)
Sadly, the billet-doux is almost extinct, having given way
to the ephemera of recorded telephone messages, faxes,
and e-mail. Besides, who needs to write a love letter
when you can buy a greeting card commemorating—in
light verse—all the milestones of romance: the first kiss,
the first quarrel, even the eventual parting?

No wonder lovers turn to ready-made sentiments.
Even novelists and poets are embarrassingly inept when
confessing real feelings to a real beloved. James Joyce's
letters to his fiancée Nora Barnacle are jejune outpourings, more befitting a moony adolescent than a magician
with words. ("When I am with you I leave aside my con-
temptuous suspicious nature. I wish I felt your head on
my shoulder. I think I will go to bed.") Then again, perhaps we should distrust a well-written love letter. The
perfectly punctuated missive with crafted sentences and
carefully chosen words may suggest that the writer was

THE TECHNIQUE OF THE LOVE AFFAIR

thinking more of his composition than his love. The heart is rarely articulate and passion is seldom grammatical.

"There is a time in one's life," writes Jane Austen, "when the post office has deep significance." Until recently, the sight of familiar handwriting had a heart-stopping effect on the recipient. The first billet-doux marked a crucial stage in the progress of a courtship: it meant that a man was willing to commit his feelings indelibly to paper.

Love letters served another, less pleasant, purpose: Much to the humiliation of the couple and the diversion of the public, they were often used as evidence in sensational divorce cases.

■ ■ ■

A real love letter is absolutely ridiculous to everyone except the writer and the recipient. The composition, which repeats the same term of endearment thirteen times on a page, has certainly no particular claim to literary art. When a man writes a love letter, dated, and fully identified by name and address, there is no question but that he is in earnest. A large number of people consider nothing so innocently endearing as love letters, read in court-room, with due attention to effect, by the counsel for the other side.

—MYRTLE REED, *The Spinster Book,* 1901

Six

■ ■ ■

Women have served all these centuries
as looking-glasses possessing the magic and
delicious power of reflecting the figure of man
at twice its natural size.

—VIRGINIA WOOLF,
A Room of One's Own, 1933

CYPRIA If you have been reading attentively, you will want to know something about the manner of arousing pursuit. The time has nearly come to discuss these things with you.

I dare say you share the common fallacy of imagining that you know, more or less definitely, the type of man likely to attract you [see "Whatever Does She See in Him?" Syndrome *at the end of this chapter*]. You are sure to be influenced in your ideas by the features of the last man who attracted you, or the man who is attracting you now, or even by the hero of a favourite novel. Naturally, you are prepossessed in favour of the traits which have beguiled you before. But men exist in such an infinite variety of types, and you yourself are found in such an infinite variety of moods or circumstances, that it is almost impossible for you to prophesy your preferences with accuracy. Most married women, for instance, will admit that their husbands do not at all resemble the beings with whom they had always pictured themselves mated. I refer to this fact merely by way of warning you to preserve an open mind as to masculine fascinations, and although I would not have you take the attitude that all are fish which come to your net, I advise

■

[1] *Men whose prestige* . . .

As early as the 1890s, guide-books alerted secretaries to the predatory tactics of the married boss. "Soon you'll be working late and he'll casually suggest a late lunch . . . [and soon] he will be confiding that his wife doesn't understand him and that he has no one to talk to." The fantasy of the typist and her employer, which has sustained many a frustrated working girl, is the Cinderella story revamped for the modern age. Elsewhere, Moore is stolidly unromantic on this point.

you not to harbour unreasonable prejudices. They may cause you to miss valuable opportunities, and, in any case, much time will be lost in the conquering of them. It is true that when you meet one in whom you discover an instant physical appeal, your prejudices—even the reasonable ones—will rapidly disperse, unless they are in his favour; but it is most desirable that you should have a keen perception of the merits of men other than those who possess this quick and dangerous allure for you.

I cannot tell you what sort of men you should aim at, but I can describe those whom you should avoid.

Men whose prestige—not moral, of course, but circumstantial—is so much greater than your own that you cannot hope to be at ease with them, much less to feel a little superior, as you really should in order to enjoy yourself.[1]

Men with whom, from one cause or another, you would always have to make the first advances to keep your love affair alive.

Men whose position is such that only a hole-and-corner sort of intimacy with them is possible. It doesn't matter if *your* position only admits of hole-and-corner intimacies: that will lend you the glamour of intrigue and unattainability, while the indignity of being kept stealthily in the background must be borne by him. Having to be concealed is a much more absurd situation for a woman than for a man, and he will soon cease to respect you if you submit to it, so take care how you begin a flirtation with anyone who dares not acknowledge you.

Lastly, men who are positively dissolute. The chances

in favour of your reclaiming a man far gone in vice are small; the chances in favour of his injuring either your reputation, or your character, or both, are great. The reclamation of wastrels and degenerates is a task you should not impose upon yourself even in the deceptive name of charity.

Now as for the men I put first in my classification—men whose prestige heavily outweighs your own—I think you have more intelligence than to imagine I meant anything of this sort: That if you are, say, a typist and your rich and important employer seems to take an interest in you, you should sternly discourage him. Not at all, for as a typist you may have beauty and wit enough to balance easily your employer's prestige of wealth and established position. But suppose yourself, with only a modest equipment of assets, feeling drawn towards someone furnished with almost everything that could excite the envy of his own sex and the admiration of yours, what chance would you have of holding him, even if you managed at first to gain his serious attention? All the skill in the world could not prevent such a man from feeling, after a time, that it was rather gracious of him to give his regard to an insignificant person like you (pray take this "you" impersonally, Saccharissa!). And then, according to his disposition, he will either turn from you to aim higher, or stand by you filled with pent-up dissatisfaction, ready to flare out volcanically at any provocation. In the meantime, your self-confidence has gradually oozed away, and as a corollary, the man acquires in your eyes an even greater importance than nature and provi-

In the more prosaic world, people tend to pair with someone like themselves. According to Helen K. Fisher in *The Anatomy of Love*, "Likes tend to marry likes—individuals of the same ethnic group, with similar physical traits and levels of education, what anthropologists call positive assortive mating." So important is this question of "likeness" that a 1946 American handbook, *How to Pick a Mate*, contains a battery of tests designed to rate the reader in, among other things, nine "important personality traits" such as conformity, flexibility, dependability, idealism, and steadiness. After adding up her score, the respondent is to give the test to "her favorite date." The closer their scores, the greater the chance for a happy marriage.

dence bestowed on him: infatuation ensues, and your life is a perfect misery until the affair falls through, and for some time after.

You will gather, then, that a nice discrimination of the amatory value of your own assets and those of others is essential to your happiness, unless you are blessed with extraordinary good fortune.

In the matter of first advances, occasionally—very, very occasionally—it is permissible for you to make them openly; you may make them more frequently if you can dexterously conceal that you are doing so; but never be so mad as to launch out upon an affair which, for reasons financial, social, or emotional, would fall through unless all the first advances came from you.

Which brings me to a very particular question. How can you set about making a man approach you with overtures tending towards love? By what means can you arouse his interest to that extent? The obvious and straightforward answer is, *Be interesting*, but that word is likely to mislead. It may tempt you to believe that you must appear sensible, well-informed, original, and so forth. This is absolutely unnecessary, and would be fatal in many cases. "A woman," said Jane Austen a century ago, "if she have the misfortune of knowing anything, should conceal it as well as she can." [2] With nine men out of ten this is more true than ever, and even men of character and intellect are just as likely to fall in love with a stupid woman as a clever one, though probably not for long. I will tell you quite bluntly the four qualities which, in conjunction with a little prestige derived from

■

[2] *"A woman," said Jane Austen a century ago . . .*

In *Pride and Prejudice,* Jane Austen shows that a nimble wit and an original mind can be alluring to the right sort of man. Just after their engagement, Darcy confesses to Elizabeth Bennet that he first loved her for the "liveliness of her mind." Austen was only too aware that such things happen only in fiction, and that Darcy—one of fiction's sexiest heros—is a thinking woman's fantasy.

beauty, fame, wealth, or other assets, will make most men notice you: poise of manner, light-heartedness, neatness of apparel, and a talent for flattery.

Your poise, of course, must be evident in freedom from embarrassed self-consciousness, and freedom as well from arrogance or clamorousness. If you cannot feel at ease, then shyness is more agreeable than over-confidence, but let your shyness be of the kind that is blushing and tremulous, not callow and clumsy. Whatever you are doing, let it be gracefully done. Don't laugh with too much abandon, for instance, throwing yourself into ungainly attitudes, as many women do. Don't become vehement and heated in discussion, for if he sees you taking any subject very seriously, he will conclude that you have thought deeply upon it, and until you have gained some hold, it is better not to show any depth. You should be able to sit and stand in perfect repose, you should also be able to grow lively without growing obstreperous. You must be willing to enter into the spirit of any good thing, and yet never get carried away, and you must be capable of displaying your accomplishments and personal allurements without seeming to call attention to them.

As to light-heartedness, you must appear, if not positively cheerful, at least free from any hint of grief or dejection.[3] An air of wistful melancholy may be interesting in men, but it is very rarely interesting *to* them. Of course, there are exceptions. A man labouring under some poignant sorrow may be so much moved by the contemplation of someone else in the same plight as to feel a sympathetic

■

[3] *As to light-heartedness . . .*
Etiquette manuals stressed the importance of at least appearing to be cheerful. Upon entering the ballroom, girls would immediately assume an expression of determined gaiety.

Monica looked at herself in a mirror, and "saw that she was wearing too serious an expression. Both her mother and the dancing-mistress had warned her about this, and she immediately assumed an air of fresh, sparkling enjoyment."
—E. M. Delafield,
Thank Heaven Fasting, 1932

■

[4]*. . . the less it resembles . . .*

Dietrich's tuxedo, Garbo's pants, and Hepburn's slacks illustrate the force of erotic androgyny. Properly worn, masculine-style attire enhances a woman's femininity merely by contrast.

The boyish look of the 1920s was really a girlish make-believe—women weren't imitating men but enticing them. But masculine attire "works" only when worn with irony and *esprit*. When women seriously adopt monocles, ties, and smoking jackets, they exude an unappealing aura.

■

[5]*. . . most women are all too ready . . .*

As an authority on costume, Moore was intrigued by the mutability of fashion, its seemingly haphazard changes from one season to the next. What made the bonnet give way to the hat? Do shoulder pads "say" anything about the status of women? What is the psycho-sexual "meaning" of the bustle? and so on. Dismissing detailed historical and psychological explanations, Moore says that styles change simply because human beings love variety. And

attraction for her, but, more often than not, misery long sustained begets pity unmingled with any element of sexual love.

Next, I have something to say on your apparel.

The vast majority of men know nothing more of women's dress than that it is flimsy and expensive, and that the less it resembles their own the more they like it [*see* Fashion, Men, and Women *at the end of this chapter*].[4] The only way an average man can tell whether you are in fashion is by observing that you are dressed more or less like all the other women he sees. If you are dressed in the same style as most other women, but somewhat more sumptuously, he will think you smart and be proud of you; but smartness in the shape of originality and distinction merely renders him uncomfortable. He fears you are making yourself conspicuous, and in his sex conspicuousness—except it be of the sort called fame—is simply "bad form." You must banish from your wardrobe anything that could be termed striking. But this counsel is scarcely needed except by the very young and the unconventional: most women are all too ready to forfeit their individuality to the prevailing mode.[5]

You may not require to be told that you must leave courageous independence in costume to other women if you seek popularity with the general run of men [*see* Flapper Fashions *at the end of this chapter*], but there is one admonition which you are pretty sure to need—and equally sure to neglect. No doubt when you wish to kindle admiration, you are in the habit of taking unlimited trouble and spending all that you can spare, in order to appear in as many different dresses—with their accompanying shoes, hats, and so forth. If only I could make you really grasp the fact that at least half of this expense and effort is utterly wasted—that by far the greatest number of males are simply not observant enough about women's clothes to notice all these changes, much less to appreciate them! I know this is hard to realise when you carry in your mind compliments upon your dress which seemed to show considerable appreciation. The men who praised you probably singled out your costume for flattering comment because they knew that no applause is more congenial to a woman than that; the appearance of discrimination was, as likely as not, accidental. If you exercise your memory impartially, you may recollect times when the same men expressed themselves charmed with what you felt were the least handsome garments in your possession.

Jane Austen is shrewd upon this topic as upon almost any other connected, directly or indirectly, with the love affair. "It would be mortifying," she says, "to the feelings of many ladies, could they be made to understand how little the heart of man is affected by what is costly or new in their attire; how little it is biased by the texture of their muslin, and how unsusceptible of peculiar tenderness towards the spotted, the sprigged, the mull, or the jackonet."

"Neatness and fashion" are, in her opinion, sufficient to gratify the masculine eye and pride. That is all we demand of men, that is all they demand of us. We do not ask that they shall be wearing different suits every time we see them, and we should scarcely notice it if they did. They too are quite free from any yearning to see us exhaust variety in

women follow fashion not because they wish to attract men but to "demonstrate, however deludedly, their independence and freedom from masculine domination." For some women wearing a backless dress is a daring act of self-assertion.

■

[6] *"it is a great comfort to be well-dressed"* . . .

Anyone who's ever suffered the embarrassment of walking into a party wearing formal wear only to confront the pitiless gaze of the casually attired can appreciate the importance of wearing the "right" clothes. Department store buyers know that Southern women wear more pastels and more makeup than their Northern counterparts, who tend to favor neutral tones and tailored styles. The iridescent blue eye shadow and "big hair," which may be *de rigueur* in Houston, are reserved for drag queens in New York.

■

[7] *If she be not groomed to perfection* . . .

Robert Herrick's poem "Delight in Disorder" celebrates a certain patrician negligence:

*A careless shoestring, in whose tie
I see a wild civility:
Do more bewitch me than when art
    Is too precise in every part.*

Herrick implies that a slight air of *déshabillé* hints that a woman might be equally casual in dispens-

our garb, and all our contrivances for being dressed differently at each meeting are squandered on beings who are capable of exclaiming, "Ha, a new frock!" about something they have seen us wear half-a-dozen times.

Nevertheless, although I deplore the habit of making strained efforts after variety in dressing, I admit with Lady Mary Wortley Montague that "it is a great comfort to be well-dressed in agreeable company,"[6] and I cannot deny that an attractive woman must needs spend a good deal of time upon the care of her person. If she be not groomed to perfection from head to foot,[7] she will lack some of the confidence in herself that is so desirable.

Later, more must be said upon this important question, but for the present we will speed on to make flattery our theme.

Every normal creature is susceptible, in some degree, to flattery. The least conceited have their soft spots for a well-turned compliment, and to really vain people even the most fulsome praise is not disgusting. It seems absurd to attempt any defence of flattery when the art, properly professed, is so obviously charming, and beneficial both to the exponent and the auditor; for does not the exponent grow benevolent through constantly saying and doing things that are genial and pleasing? and does not the person for whom these pleasant and genial things are said and done blossom out to his fullest and best under their warming influence? But the art *must* be properly professed. Mere "blarney" is unpardonable, while, on the other hand, too much emotion and sincerity defeat your ends.

To begin with an elementary rule,[8] you must always seem attentive to his conversation; conceal the signs of flagging interest at any cost, but yet don't look too eagerly engrossed, or he will soon feel his talk is so delightful to you that he does you rather a favour by talking at all. Equally elementary, but highly effective, is the well-known policy of drawing a man out to speak about himself. Take warning, however, against one grave error. Encourage a man to speak of himself, by all means, but at first only in a light and superficial manner. Never attempt to probe the secret places of his heart without considerable evidence that he wants you to do so; for even though he may be glad to pour his confidence into your ears—which will not invariably be the case—he will regard you more as a friend than as a woman to be pursued. And it is irritating to be looked upon as a confidential friend, and neglected accordingly, by a man you long to captivate. Let him then reveal the whole surface of his life to you if he pleases, but make no attempt on your own initiative to pierce beneath it. Neither should your flattery take the form of giving him your own confidence in any but small things. You must not let him be privy to either the best or the worst of your character and circumstances until you are secure of his affection.

Now comes a rule less elementary, more difficult to put into practice. It is the very corner-stone of the true technique, and I should like to impress it upon you forcibly. *Be more complimentary in your speech than in your attitude.* While your actions are well-controlled, and seem biassed rather towards indifference than infatuation, you can afford

ing her sexual favors. An overly meticulous look, one that is perfectly correct as to color, fashion, and design, suggests an overly-organized mind and, perhaps, a fear of losing control. Whereas dirt and slovenliness are always taboo, clothes worn with negligent grace (such as an insouciant drop of a shoulder strap) can be just as artful—and more ravishing—than a creation from the most celebrated Parisian couturier.

■

[8] *To begin with an elementary rule . . .*

In *You Just Don't Understand: Men and Women in Conversation* (1990), the linguist Deborah Tannen observes that men tend to communicate by "holding forth" in conversations consisting of lectures or factual explanations. The speaker (male) assumes the superior position of mentor, while the listener (female) is the appreciative pupil. Conversational styles begin early: Starting in adolescence, girls are told that if they want to be popular with boys, they'll have to become what is known in dating manuals as "a good listener."

■

Lady Mary Wortley Montagu[e]:
   Mary Montague (1689–1762) was an indefatigable traveler, feminist, poet, letter writer, and essayist. Few people are aware that she introduced the English to the practice of inoculating against smallpox.
   She was a strong female presence in a predominantly masculine literary world, and in an age known for its clever badinage, she could hold her own with the likes of Alexander Pope. As this couplet from "The Lover" demonstrates, her verse is both witty and down to earth: "But when the long hours of public are past,/ "And we meet, with champagne and a chicken, at last." . . . More than a century later, the poet Byron would write admiringly, "What say you to such a supper with such a woman?"

to be somewhat generous with your words. I don't mean that you should be effusive, or make false promises, or pretend you feel more than you do. Quite the reverse.

   If you are always flattering a man, both in word and deed, he will soon see that you want him badly, and he will cease to pursue. If you are always cold and casual, both in word and deed, he will think you don't want him at all, and a passion does not flourish long when rebuffed at every turn. It is necessary, therefore, for you to find a line of conduct through which he will receive as much flattery as will encourage him, and as many anxieties about your state of mind as will make you seem elusive. Countless women think to achieve this by the appalling practice of being rude in their speech and yet complaisant in their every act. They imagine that impoliteness conceals the ardour which would otherwise be evinced by their complaisance. They accept invitations with a vulgar affectation of "don't-care-whether-I-do-or-I-don't," they take gifts without any seemly appearance of pleasure, they think they are "giving themselves away" if they allow anything visibly to impress them, they tell a man painful truths about himself. But still they are there whenever he wants them, and if he becomes neglectful, they soon take steps to recall themselves to his mind. No amount of rudeness will hide these facts, and so their lovers see them to be just as undesirably easy of access and far more disagreeable than if they were as obliging in speech as in practice.

   The best plan is to spare no kindness that the tongue can utter—except confessions of love, jealousy, and so forth, which, while they gratify him, deprive you of prestige.

Beyond these omissions, scarcely any amiability is too great. You should never disdain even to express a few trifling insincerities when not to do so might inflict a wound. You will be more attractive, for example, pretending to be pleased with an inappropriate gift than showing your dissatisfaction, and besides that, he will be stimulated by your appreciation to get you other gifts—and the more he gives you, the more he will love you. Say charming things, but restrain your impulses to do them; be prettily grateful for an invitation, but not too eager to accept it; express yourself as glad to see him, but show no great desire for his company in any of your actions. This attitude, carried into all your dealings, will keep him in just that condition of suspense and bewilderment which is—at least in the beginning—so necessary.

The last rule of flattery I will give you here is to let a man feel superior to you in all the matters in which his sex takes especial pride. You may not like to be regarded as weak, nervous, and inconsistent, but man has always looked on strength of body and mind as his prerogative, and to usurp it would make you unlovable in his eyes. What matter, therefore, if he smile at you for your weakness and softness, your capricious moods, and silly clothes, and ignorance of the topics of the day, when the knowledge of his having the advantage of you fills him with chivalry and adoration? It is the acme of folly to attempt to compete with him on his own ground. If you keep up with him it is enough—perhaps more than enough.

Let him beat you at games, let him order your dinner when he takes you to a restaurant, let him laugh at your

The writer Jean Giraudoux recognized the potency and efficacy of flattery: In his play *The Apollo of Bellac*, he writes: "When you see a woman who can go nowhere without a staff of admirers, it is not so much because they think she's beautiful, it is because she has told them they are handsome."

politics, and shake his head over your logic.[9] Give him every opportunity of seeing how feeble you are wherever he habitually excels. Each of your blunders will endear you to him.

When he is with you, let him feel strong, courageous, generous, and he will behave like a paladin to you. If you show him that you expect him to be a cad, then a cad he will be. Men will give you whatever you seem to ask of them.

Ask much.

The "Whatever Does She See in Him?" Syndrome

I dare say you share the common fallacy . . . (p. 77)
Scientists should call the enigma of desire the "Whatever Does She See in Him?" syndrome. In *A Midsummer Night's Dream*, Shakespeare captures the strangeness of love and the mysteries and inanities it engenders. Under the influence of a magic spell, Titania, the fairy queen, falls head over heels in love with an ass (a donkey, that is). What Shakespeare seems to say is that romantic love is a form of enchantment that transforms an ass into an Adonis. When the spell fades and clarity is restored, we, like Titania, shudder and dismiss it as a waking dream.

What we saw was the elusive phantom we call our "type," which, lodged deep in our brains, is a portrait of our ideal lover, a hodgepodge of desirable attributes we've assembled unconsciously through the years. We're wired to fall in love with anyone who resembles this paragon.

Why, for instance, does one woman have a "thing" for short men with Slavic features? What circuitry signals the brain "This is it!" The answer may lie in childhood. The sexologist John Money proposes that somewhere between the ages of five and eight we create a "love map," a pattern based on experiences—the pharmacist who gave us candy, a curly-haired woman who smiled on a bus—that contribute to the creation of the map. A composite slowly emerges, based on feelings and qualities we found pleasing. In adolescence the map assumes its final shape, becoming, Money writes, "quite specific as to details of the physiognomy, build, race, and color of the ideal lover, not to mention temperament, manners and so on."

The image of the Ideal is not sculpted in marble and is far more malleable than we think. People have fallen for—and happily married—an anti-type. In *Remembrance of Things Past*, Swann falls deeply in love with Odette, a woman who is nothing like his usual type. Years of obsession and jealousy follow, and then, cured of his delusion, he awakens one morning and exclaims, "To think that I've wasted years of my life, that I've longed to die, that I've experienced my greatest love, for a woman who didn't appeal to me, who wasn't even my type!"

We tend to justify passion by justifying our
love objects: Christopher, George, or Jerry
is uniquely worthy of our love. We like to

believe our feeling is a reasonable response to an external provocation—the excellence of Christopher, Jerry, or George. We prefer to ignore the extent to which our spontaneous and perhaps ludicrous love has irradiated and transformed Christopher or Jerry.

—PHYLLIS ROSE,
"Seamus in Love," from
Never Say Goodbye, 1991

■ ■ ■

Fashion, Men, and Women

Whether it was the first cause or not, from the
earliest times one important function of clothing
was to promote erotic activity: to attract men and
women to one another, thus ensuring the survival
of the species. One basic purpose of costume,
therefore, is to distinguish men from women.

—ALISON LURIE,
The Language of Clothes, 1981

■ ■ ■

The vast majority of men . . . (p. 82)
Male indifference to female fashion is legendary, the stuff
of *New Yorker* cartoons. The stock response "Is that what
they're wearing this year?" is usually uttered with toler-
ant amusement, as if the male speaker were above the
whimsy of fashion. The message is clear: Real men don't
know a camisole from a caftan. But it's safe to say that a

slinky gown sends an entirely different signal to the masculine brain than a pair of baggy pants.

One of the first functions of clothing, aside from providing protection from the elements, was to distinguish between the sexes. Human females don't engage in intricate mating dances or flaunt glorious plumage to advertise their availability but choose their clothing to accomplish the same purpose.

"Feminine" attire tends to be anything flimsy, voluminous, revealing, constricting—and uncomfortable. The "repressed" Victorian gentlewoman wore a bustle to emphasize her buttocks, while the "liberated" woman of the 1960s sported a tube top and a tight miniskirt. One was burdened by forty pounds of corset, bustle, and crinoline; the other wore only two strips of cloth. Neither could move with ease, but that wasn't the point. Each garment increased its wearer's odds in the mating game.

Encumbering attire is seductive because it renders a woman pleasingly helpless. Clothing that's unsuitable for labor is like a mandarin's long fingernails, a subtle boast of well-bred idleness. Constricting garments indicate her privileged yet inferior status.

The looser, more comfortable fashions of today reflect women's liberation from the sexual and economic constraints of the past. The girdle of the 1950s is as obsolete as the bustle. Yet uncomfortable, seductive attire will never go completely out of style because women, at least some of the time, dress to attract men, and durable sports-wear will never replace a lacy bustier. The two express a woman's disparate, sometimes conflicting, roles.

When a woman looks in the closet and asks, "What shall I wear?" she is essentially asking, "Whom shall I be?" But no matter what she chooses, she inescapably reveals something about herself. And a man, no matter how much he professes indifference to a woman's attire, decodes the clues and meanings in her attire.

Take shoes, for instance. The Oxford is the Eleanor Roosevelt of footwear: durable, utilitarian, and dowdy. The Manolo Blahnik sling-back is the Jean Harlow—useless, beautiful, and expensive. Women may have come a long way, but the ones who made the greatest strides probably wore sensible shoes. The others minced along behind—probably on the arm of a man.

Whether trashy red stilettos or elegant black pumps, high heels are the archetypal symbol of sex appeal. They were first worn in the fifteenth century by Venetian streetwalkers who used the heel's distinctive clicking sound to signal their availability. Even today they retain a vestige of their original purpose, hinting at a sexual invitation that may or may not be intended. (During the 1890s it was fashionable for intoxicated gentlemen to toast one another with high-heeled slippers filled with Champagne.)

High heels make legs look shapelier; walking in them arches the back, tilts the buttocks, and pushes the bust out, a primitive gesture of courtship from the savanna to the singles bar. That high heels attract men is reason enough for most women to endure the agony—and the injury—they inflict. And they flatter men because they imply that the wearer is willing to sacrifice her comfort for his pleasure.

Clothes are a discreet accoutrement to an intriguing woman, not a sandwich board of sexual self-promotion. Almost any woman can attract male attention by wearing a see-through blouse, but it takes technique—and confidence—to attract without flaunting. Cypria's idea that women should be aloof yet potentially available translates into sensuous clothing that conceals as it reveals, dress that suggests that its wearer *might* be available to the right man—*if* she so chooses. If clothing makes a statement, then the ideal outfit would be somewhere between a rebuff and an invitation.

No wonder a woman who dresses with flair
makes a big impression. It doesn't have to be a
major fashion offensive, either. . . . A good
fashion sense is like a good sense of humor,
or a clever fresh way of phrasing things.

—WILLIAM GRIMES,
New York Times, 1994

■ ■ ■

Flapper Fashions

You may not require to be told . . . (p. 82)

Young women of the 1920s saw themselves as sartorial rebels. The fashion industry, dormant during the war, suddenly revived, compressing sixteen years' worth of changes into six. New styles emerged: The popularity of the American cocktail naturally led to the creation of a cocktail dress. Throughout the decade, hemlines, that trusty gauge of public sentiment, rose, dropped, rose, dropped, and rose again. In 1928, skirts stopped above the knee, the highest ever, and would never return to their prewar length.

There were other innovations: The short, narrow skirt gave working women a smart, crisp look, and, according to Hollander, provided the visual coherence of male attire. Under former sartorial regimes, most women adopted the uniform of the Lady—gloves, hat, ankle-length gown, petticoats, corset. The modern woman's closet was a miscellany of styles, each with a matching personality: audacious, businesslike, droll, or sultry. For the first time, clothes could be witty.

That ageless flapper Coco Chanel led the way, spreading her mania for tanning and dieting. Her models, slender, active, and young, would become the female prototype for the next seven decades. Bosomless, hipless, and bottomless, they inspired the shift and the jumper, low-waisted garments that skimmed the body and ended at mid-calf. These linear dresses emphasized the angular elegance of the female shape.

The slender, even skinny *gamine* look was quintessential Jazz Age chic. With scarlet lips and a cloche hat slouched over her brow, the modern girl seemed impudent and stylish, not at all masculine. The street urchin by day transformed herself into a vamp by night. Evening wear, sophisticated and sinuous, clung to the flesh like wet drapery, a far cry from the billowing white muslin of an earlier age. Black, once reserved for men, the religious, and mourning, was the *dernier cri* in modern glamour. Sequins, spangles, appliqués, pearls, beads, and fringes created textures that begged to be touched.

The young woman of 1925 looks more like us than her Victorian mother. Her hair was short and loose, her body slender, her hemline at the knee. Liberated from the corset, the modern girl could move with a fluidity that allowed her to feel her body's suppleness.

Seven

■ ■ ■

Men and women who are too aggressive at the
beginning of the courting process . . .
suffer unpleasant consequences. If you come
too close, touch too soon, or talk too much,
you will probably be repelled. Like wooing
among wolf spiders, baboons, and
many creatures, the human pickup runs on
messages. At every juncture in the ritual each
partner must respond correctly, otherwise
the courtship fails.

—HELEN K. FISHER,
The Anatomy of Love, 1992

SACCHARISSA Well, Cypria, I have read all that you have written until now, and I confess to a strong desire to know how you would set about it if you intended to make anyone your pursuer.

CYPRIA What to do, when you first decide to make a man like you, I *can* tell you, but only in the rough. If I wanted to go into detail, it would mean writing an enormous series of volumes, with chapter headings something like this: "How to Attract a Handsome Stranger who has Just Helped to Start up your Frozen Car," "How to Attract a Man Whom you Meet again after Several Years during which he has been Married and Divorced," and so on. No, no, I can only deal with attraction on general lines. You want to know how to awaken interest—well, on general lines I will tell you, but first I must make one presumption, and that is that the man you decide upon is not already engrossed in some other woman.

SACCHARISSA If you mean me personally, I can assure you I should never seek to inveigle any other woman's cavalier away from her.

CYPRIA Come, don't be sanctimonious.[1] There are occasions when you might wean a man from a previous attachment without the slightest cause for self-reproach.

■

[1] *Come, don't be sanctimonious.*
  Cypria's rebuke lies at the heart of Moore's philosophy. Throughout her long life Moore viewed abstract idealism and sentimentality as the enemy of reason. The average person, she insists, will unthinkingly adopt an inherited sense of decorum, and will do anything to avoid unpleasant truths and the complexity of experience.

But as a rule, it is certainly pleasanter, as well as easier, to confine oneself to such as are free. Now your technique will differ according to whether the man you deem worthy of conquest is a new acquaintance, or one you have never met at all, or one whom you know well. I shall deal with each in turn, beginning with the man you have just met. He is rather a dangerous fellow, because your having felt drawn towards him from the beginning indicates that for you he possesses that animal magnetism which is likely to mislead.

SACCHARISSA   If I am so especially susceptible to it in his case, surely it is clear that he is a congenial type for me, and therefore not dangerous?

CYPRIA   Why, that is the gravest error you could make. The fact that someone happens to awaken one of your perhaps unrecognised primitive appetites should never be taken as evidence of his suitability for you. But let me return to my subject—where was I?

SACCHARISSA   You were supposing me about to attempt the conquest of someone I had just met.

CYPRIA   Well, your first care will be to remember that any appearance of haste in using your blandishments is unseemly and may defeat your purpose.[2] Avoid singling a man out for special glances and special flattery, unless you know you will have no later opportunity.

SACCHARISSA   What if he singles me out first?

CYPRIA   In that case you may congratulate yourself. An effortless conquest naturally means that for him at least you have physical appeal.

SACCHARISSA   But you said that was dangerous!

CYPRIA   For you, if he has it; for him, if you have it.

---

[2] *Well, your first care . . .*
The first few moments of a potential affair are fraught with hidden peril. Just about anything can destroy a budding romance: a raucous, snorting laugh, florid perfume, gaudy jewelry. Everyone has a pet peeve that kills any thought of romance, no matter how "nice" the other person seems. Since the prospective partner can't assimilate these "flaws" into a larger context, he or she tends to be unforgiving. The anonymous She or He is reduced to an offending laugh or smell. Conversely, as an affair progresses, lovers tend to excuse even the most egregious lapses.

That's another thing. But if you can win him without effort, dear Saccharissa, you scarcely require to be told any methods of arousing pursuit, so let us not assume anything so facile.

SACCHARISSA Very well, I will picture myself desiring to captivate the man without his having made a single overture.

CYPRIA Good. And we are agreed that you will not be hasty while there is any likelihood of seeing him again. At your second or third meeting, however, some encouragement is not amiss.

SACCHARISSA What shape should it take?

CYPRIA Flattering deference is rather good, I think, at the beginning. A man is always glad of praise, even when he can see through your motive for it. In fact, at this stage you may deliberately let him see your motive—with subtlety of course—and you will not be making a blunder. What really flatters him is that you think him worth flattering. He will only gather that you want to flirt, whereas if he were allowed to imagine that your appreciation flowed from the fullness of your heart, he might form a much more serious notion of your feelings, and one which would detract from your power. I believe that to appear practised in the more elegant kinds of flirtation will increase rather than impair your status with him, because it implies that you are accustomed to the attentions of men.

SACCHARISSA Perhaps he will merely think that I set my cap at any man.

CYPRIA If he is normal, his vanity will not let him form that conclusion without unmistakable proofs. Even if you

■

³ *. . . you must pretend that some obstacle . . .*

It is almost axiomatic that a lover's interest will be piqued by the denial of access to the love object. Psychologists call this the Romeo and Juliet effect.

In Western culture the virginity taboo provided the ultimate obstacle, and thus made the forbidden virgin all the more desirable.

I spent three or four months . . . becoming everyday more amorous, for the reason that every day I ran upon a new obstacle that I had myself created.

—Benjamin Constant,
The Red Note Book
(1907)

actually were that kind of person, he would not readily discover it; for a little while, at least, he would firmly believe that he was different from other men in your eyes, and that your advances were due to his own particular charm. No, no, he will like you and not disrespect you for letting him see, after a few encounters with him, a hint of sexual interest in your manner; but, mark this, it must be no more than a hint. I had better put it this way: you may betray your *wish* to flirt, but not your *willingness.*

SACCHARISSA   That sounds subtle. How could I do it?

CYPRIA   With perfect ease. You must show, as I say, that you are interested in him, but when he first seeks to make you express your interest in words or caresses, you must pretend that some obstacle impedes your complete response.³

SACCHARISSA   Can you suggest any suitable obstacles?

CYPRIA   Yes, from within there are modesty, shyness, caprice, conventionality, and so forth: from without, there are the jealousies of other men—

SACCHARISSA   What if there are none to be jealous?

CYPRIA   You may invent them—not in so many words, for lying is bad policy, but by innuendo. You would never be such a fool, I hope, as to let him know quite definitely that there were no other men. Then there is Mrs. Grundy in all her guises;⁴ she is a splendid obstacle, one to rouse the spirit of any sensible man. Excellent creature, where should we be without her!

SACCHARISSA   When you said that I should not make a *complete* response, did you mean to imply that *some* response might be permitted?

CYPRIA I did. As long as you do not respond as much as he would like—as long as you almost seem to be doing so under protest (not the protest of disinclination, mark you, but of modesty, or conventionality, or any other obstacle you may have chosen), you might make a little show of surrender.

SACCHARISSA And that is called coquetry, I suppose. How long must I go on with that kind of thing?

CYPRIA Almost for ever, I am afraid. You dare not cease to give a little less of yourself than is wanted, a little less than satisfies, save on the rarest occasions, and those should decidedly be foreign to the period of approach.

SACCHARISSA What should I do if, in spite of propinquity and all my arts, he were to pay no attention to me?

CYPRIA You should give up the endeavour without compromise, and in the future any advance which is ever made should come from him. If an unattached man is indifferent to your flattery, he is indifferent to you.

SACCHARISSA Perhaps he dislikes mere flirtation, and his position will not allow of serious intentions.

CYPRIA A saccharine notion, Saccharissa. There may be men who dislike "mere flirtation" and coldly ignore a woman who attracts them, but you will have to look for them in monasteries and other retired places. No ordinary man will wait until he has matrimony in view before he begins to make love to you. It is generally only in the course of a light affair that the serious one springs up.

SACCHARISSA And now, Cypria, let me ask you what I am to do when I meet a man whom it is not probable that

■

4 *...Mrs. Grundy...*
A personage mentioned but never seen in Thomas Morton's 1798 comedy *Speed the Plough.* The refrain "What will Mrs. Grundy think?" echoes through the play. Her name has become synonymous with narrow-minded public opinion:

They eat, and drink, and scheme, and plod,
And go to sleep on Sunday—
And many are afraid of God—
And more of Mrs. Grundy.
—Frederick Locker-Lampson,
"The Jester," 1857

■

5. *. . . stoop to getting to know strangers?*

Saccharissa's surprise shows how insular society was, whereas Cypria's rebuke marks a new social attitude—and the beginning of the progress to the 1970s and the advent of singles clubs, dating services, and personal ads. For the gentry, the England of the 1920s was a private club in which everyone knew or had heard of everyone else. Social registers such as Debrett's were indispensable in locating a stranger's family and background on the social map. Strangers were outsiders. For a certain segment of society, picking up a stranger in a gallery or train, as Saccharissa proposes, could prove dangerous—not because he might be part of the white slave trade but because he might be *in* trade.

The war, however, enlarged a woman's social sphere, introducing her to people she would never have met otherwise. That, in addition to the scarcity of eligible men, made her more willing to consider those once deemed ineligible. As standards relaxed, the importance of birth, background, and breeding declined and would continue to do so through the century.

I shall see again unless I make an impression on him at once—someone who does not mix with my friends, and who is not associated with any of my business.

CYPRIA   In short, a chance acquaintance.

SACCHARISSA   Not necessarily.

CYPRIA   No, you are right, some men whom you meet through orthodox introduction may not be likely to cross your path again. But why do you look askance upon chance acquaintanceship? Surely it shows a more independent spirit to strike out for yourself and enlarge your practice ground. Besides, in many ways it is more convenient; you avoid the tacit conflict with your friends which is liable to arise when a man whom they knew first, and consider as their peculiar property, becomes attached to you. And then, suppose he should do something which might make you wish to see no more of him—how much easier it would be to drop a chance acquaintance than one whose life is interlinked with your everyday affairs.

SACCHARISSA   But surely you don't imagine I should ever deliberately stoop to getting to know strangers?[5]

CYPRIA   Come, come, my dear girl, one day even I shall lose patience with you! Where is the degradation in one human being wanting contact with another—and taking steps towards it too, if necessary? It is a particularly narrow snobbery, that pretence of never wishing to know anybody whom you do not already know.

But to continue. You want to know how you can create at a first meeting an impression which will make a man try to see you again. Well, except when circumstances are very favourable, it is a difficult thing to manage without some momentary loss of prestige.

If you are skilful, it will be very, very slight indeed, and you can make it up later. Where a slow and measured method would be unavailing, you must be prepared to take a trifling risk. You see, in order to rouse interest in an indifferent stranger, you must not only address him in a seductive fashion, but you must be generally striking and amusing, and it is an odd truth that when a woman appears thus to the average man, she repels even while she attracts.

SACCHARISSA How so?

CYPRIA I think it due to the masculine dislike of conspicuous people.

SACCHARISSA Am I not then conspicuous when I am greatly in demand, which you said would be an advantage?

CYPRIA Yes, but popularity, like fame, is a thing men don't distrust. You are as it were hallmarked with the approval of others, and warranted genuine as a desirable female. But at this first meeting we are not counting on his being able to rate you at anybody else's valuation. You have come across him, perhaps, in a hotel, on a train, or, say, at a party, at which you are being neither more nor less sought after than the other guests. He shows no sign of particularly noticing you, so you must find a way of forcing his attention, and in as agreeable a manner as possible. Your best looks, your most graceful attitudes, your most accomplished talk, your airiest ripostes—you must bring them all to your aid. They will undoubtedly awaken a spark of interest (always assuming that the man's interest is not deeply engaged elsewhere), and the spark can be fanned to flame by introducing into your conversation a delicately personal note, the subtle play upon his egoism. Be sophisticated and wonderfully feminine. Be elegant and a little spoiled, but not bored. Be light, amiable, quite dissociated from care and all the common things of life. You will fascinate him enough to make him want your company again, but he will not like you very much, and so you will have to expend considerable skill in the future to correct his first impressions. Your sophistication, adroitness, and apparent hedonism will make a voluptuous appeal; but he will feel the faint antagonism that nearly the whole conscience-stricken race of men feels towards sensually pleasing things; also, he will think you are probably "bad form."

SACCHARISSA But if I seem elegant, and accomplished, how can he think that?

CYPRIA My dear girl, those are exactly the points that will make him think so. Did you ever see an Englishwoman in "*good* form" who was exquisite and alluring [*see* The Dowdy Englishwoman *at the end of this chapter*]? Are they not all stiff, and clumsy, and devoid of smartness? Why, elegance is almost indecent in a county family!

SACCHARISSA Do you recommend, then, that later on I become stiff and clumsy to show him that I am "good form" after all?

CYPRIA Not so, for when he finds you are likable as well as noticeable, he will simply forget about form, or find yours exemplary.

SACCHARISSA I don't believe I should ever wish to

captivate anyone who was snob enough to think about such a trivial matter in the first place.

CYPRIA Then you intend to confine your regard to most exceptional men. Perhaps it is not so much a question of snobbery as of the desire for conformity. The average man is afraid of originality.[6] He adheres with rigid orthodoxy to the standards of the class with which he identifies himself, in manners, dress, vocabulary, and even thought. If he belongs to the class which hunts hares and stags and foxes to death for pleasure, then, however humane nature may have meant him to be, he will manage to convince himself that it's all very sporting and grand, and that anyone who says it isn't is beneath consideration; if he belongs to the class which calls itself Bohemian, then he will be unconventional after the best conventional method. And in every stratum of society a man—an average man—subconsciously desires womenfolk who will conform to the standards which are considered pleasing by the majority of his acquaintances, and thereby do him credit. Bear in mind that I said "womenfolk," meaning to imply those with whom he has long and serious relationships; in his little interludes he will tolerate, and even like, the unusual, though he will still be distrustful of it.

SACCHARISSA I should never enjoy being treated as a little interlude.

CYPRIA I agree. There are many reasons why it is permissible for a woman to look upon a man in that light if she pleases, yet she cannot afford to be so looked upon herself. But sometimes you must present yourself in the guise of

■

[6] *The average man is afraid of originality.*

The author of a husband-hunting manual from the 1980s assured readers they'd be married in a year if they adopted the style of the man they wished to attract. Thus if you want to catch a stockbroker, don't shave your head or pierce any body part other than the ears, and be advised that scholars rarely fall for women who look like they fit in at the Grand Ole Opry. Yet an inspired touch, an element of surprise, is always delightful. A pair of earrings from Tibet, antique lace, or a Garboesque cloche hat worn with a sedate suit might well invite a second look.

Cecil was still young enough to wish to be different from other people, while desiring still more, like all Englishmen, to appear as much as possible like everybody else.
—Ada Leverson,
The Little Ottleys, 1908–16

one who offers brief diversion, in order to gain attention rapidly where otherwise you might never gain it at all. Afterwards, each time you meet him you must bring into evidence more and more the qualities which will make for prestige in his eyes, and suppress those which will deprive you of it. By the time he would have been giving you up if you had really been a mere diversion, he will start to fall in love with you in earnest.

SACCHARISSA It all sounds very plausible, but I cannot believe that all men respond in the same way to the same artifices.

CYPRIA Not *all,* certainly, but as large a proportion as would justify my statements. I admit there are numerous exceptions. Some men are comparatively free from the fetters of self-consciousness and care little for the world's opinion, and some are of such great importance that they can almost afford to ignore it: others, very young ones as a rule, take a pride in shocking the world, and love to be seen about with what Mr. George Robey[7] used to call "a lady of promiscuous allurements." But no man is entirely uninfluenced by a woman's effect upon the rest of his sex, and even the sensational youth of nineteen or twenty steadies down in a few years to an axe-grinding citizen who wants to stand well with his fellow creatures. I believe that nine men out of ten will react to your artifices as long as they are not in love with another woman at the time, or are not of a character and habits utterly antipathetic to your own.

SACCHARISSA True, but I should like to ask—

CYPRIA No, dear Saccharissa, I beg you won't. If all

■

7. ... *Mr. George Robey* ...

In *Muddling Through* (1936), a comic guide to Britain, Theodora Benson and Betty Askwith include George Robey on their roster of quintessential English personalities. He is, they write, "the Prime Minister of Mirth. He demonstrates good broad vulgar fun in a dignified British way. He has (detachable) eyebrows."

my counsel is to be remembered by you, as I should wish, you must not take too much of it at a time.

SACCHARISSA But we have not even exhausted the topic of my effect on new acquaintances, and we have still to deal with the men who belong to other categories.

CYPRIA Yes, let us talk of them to-morrow. The personal variations of what we have been discussing are, I imagine, considerable enough to occupy your mind until then.

The Dowdy Englishwoman

Did you ever see an Englishwoman ... (p. 108)
The peculiarly English aversion to anything extravagant
or chic produced a style best described as anti-fashion, or
"dowdy." Indeed, the personification of dowdiness is the
Queen herself, clad in a shapeless mac, a scarf knotted
under her chin, clutching the ubiquitous handbag.

The upper-class Englishwoman's proximity to stables
and kennels made delicate or feminine attire impractical.
Apparel suggestive of outdoor pursuits thus became the
signature "look" of the blue-blooded woman. Another
style, called "shabby genteel," is composed of traditional, well-worn, well-made attire that declares good
taste, old family, and indifference to anything faddish.
The style can't be cultivated, imitated, or bought. It signifies breeding and class, and it separates the *arrivistes*
from the old line.

The look of the sensible Englishwoman probably
originated with Queen Victoria, who even as a young
woman insisted on plain, serviceable bonnets as opposed

to flamboyant hats. In *Queen Victoria's Secrets* (1996), Adrienne Munich argues that Victoria put her Hanoverian homeliness to good use by plain dressing; her "non-style" indicated a rejection of the Regency's foppishness and moral laxity while proving her own "democracy and religion of earnestness." After the death of Prince Albert, the Queen wore only widow's weeds, attire that would make anyone feel vulgar. To be unstylish came to be stylish. In *Victoria: An Intimate Biography* (1987), Stanley Weintraub remarks that the Queen's failure to dress à la mode made her a ruler for the people; it was, he adds, "an endearing characteristic created by default."

Eight

∎ ∎ ∎

The myth of the passive female persisted in the
biological sciences well past the middle
of the twentieth century. . . . Among many
species of primates, for example, including the
mountain gorilla, gelada baboon, and brown
capuchin monkey, females initiate the majority
of copulations. Sometimes female solicitations
are subtle—a gesture such as a flick of the
tongue, a head shake, or a simple approach.

——MARY BATTEN, *Sexual Strategies,* 1992

SACCHARISSA I should like to ask a question. You recollect all those flatteries and seductions which you recommended to me. It seems to me that unless I am favoured with an opportunity of being alone with my prospective admirer, I have very little hope of practising them, and that your suggestions are of more limited application than you appear to imagine.

CYPRIA Oh no, not if you are really expert. It is wonderful what practice will enable you to do, even under the most dispiriting of all conditions.

SACCHARISSA And what is that?

CYPRIA In my opinion, your least promising position is when you must attempt to make your seductive impression in front of just one or two other people, and when those are of your own sex. You would be justified then in complaining, in an expressive colloquial phrase, that your style was cramped. There is nothing like the jealous, or disapproving, or even critical, eye of another female for disturbing your technique. But when you are sufficiently experienced, you can turn this hindrance to your advantage. Play up to the women, sparkle at them, let them be the recipients of your provocative remarks, your charming smiles, and draw the man into your conversation almost imperceptibly as you go along.

SACCHARISSA How would that serve me?

CYPRIA In this way—you are revealing yourself in just as attractive a light as you could if you were alone with him, the other women are making admirable foils to you (unless they're cleverer than you are), and you will have advanced quite a long way without committing yourself to the slightest overture.

SACCHARISSA What of the rest of my audience? They —or she—will be aware that a change has come over my personality, for I do not usually scintillate so brightly, and they will guess what I am about.

CYPRIA If you are truly an adept, you will make it your business to be very near your best with everybody, always. Then there will be no visible difference in your manner when you are observed with someone who especially pleases you. I don't recommend you to be *quite* at your best all the time, because you must have a few reserves to draw upon, but you would find it very detrimental indeed to be known as a woman who could only shine for men.

SACCHARISSA Yes, I can readily believe that large success in amatory affairs belongs to those who are liked by their own sex as well as the other.

CYPRIA Of course. Women possess sons, and brothers, and male friends, and have it in their power to be either useful or disagreeable according to the feeling you inspire in them.

SACCHARISSA Tell me, Cypria, what must I do should the spectators be, not women, but men?

CYPRIA That would be a peculiarly happy situation, as easy to manage as the other is difficult. If a woman cannot captivate when she is alone in a little group of two or three men, then there must be something radically amiss with her. I know of no company more exhilarating. Your course is clear: you must be vividly delightful and personal with each of them, drawing as much notice of a complimentary sort as you can, so that the one whom you wish to attract gets his first impression of you as a charming creature, admired and courted. On this occasion, don't single him out for any particular attention unless you can do so without their perceiving it. When a man sees that you are more interested in some other person present than in himself, his vanity is hurt, and he loses interest in you—that is, if he is not already in love with you, or tending to become so.

SACCHARISSA And, of course, if he is utterly indifferent to me, his behaviour will not contribute to my prestige. I am beginning to master your theories. But what if he should be in love with me?

CYPRIA Then your prospects of attracting the other man are still further improved. The one who is already attached to you will, by his jealousy or attentiveness, confirm your desirability to the other, on the principle which I have described; and what is more, his own passion will be enlivened when he sees you addressing your graces to someone else.

SACCHARISSA That can be no great advantage to me,

if I care for him so little that I seek to enmesh others in his very presence.

CYPRIA In the first place, dear Saccharissa, that is no proof that you do not care for him. The eagerness for conquest does not die because you achieve a victory. You may cherish the booty you have won, but you still turn in search of new triumphs. In the second place, whether you reciprocate or not, admiration must always be useful, unless your admirer be discreditable to you. When there are none to do homage, your self-confidence diminishes, and your status in worldly eyes is lowered, so it is decidedly of advantage to preserve the appreciation of your followers.

SACCHARISSA You have advised me as to my conduct before both feminine and masculine onlookers; it is time to know how I should proceed if my inclination were for a man whom I met in an ordinary mixed group of people. But in a small group where there are both women and men, to whom should I direct my attention? Should I placate the women or charm the men?

CYPRIA It is all a matter of being so exquisitely kind to the women, that your pleasantness to the men does not stand out. If there should happen to be someone present who, from rivalry or another cause, is especially disposed to resent you, be extremely amiable to her, and distinguish her by all the courtesy you can show.

SACCHARISSA Yet my purpose must be ill-natured enough if I am trying to allure a man at whom she too aims!

CYPRIA Why not? There must be competition between women.[1] That is what makes us beautiful and cultivated, and adds zest to our relationships with men and with each

■

[1] *There must be competition . . .*
As the cynic—and part-time misogynist—H. L. Mencken said, "When women kiss it always reminds one of prize fighters shaking hands."

other. And there is no harm, surely, in attempting to secure a man's affection before someone else does so, as long as you don't cheat.

SACCHARISSA Is it not cheating to disarm my opponent with fair words?

CYPRIA No, that is in accordance with the strictest rules of diplomacy. It is a polished and correct proceeding, and if she is a worthy rival, she will be as agreeable to you as you are to her, with the same intention.

SACCHARISSA What then constitutes cheating?

CYPRIA Chiefly, I think, any endeavour to deprive a woman of the affection she has already secured. When she has fairly won, she should be allowed—save in exceptional circumstances—to enjoy her victory; and I am concerned with the rule, not the exception.

SACCHARISSA I was about to ask you—how can I use that "delicate personal note" which you think so valuable, when I am under the scrutiny of others? In such a case it would be merely embarrassing, I should think.

CYPRIA To you, perhaps, but not to the man at whom your little beguilements are directed. Whatever his degree of modesty, he will not revolt against the interest of an attractive woman attractively displayed. Your showing it in the presence of others merely adds to the flattery. But, of course, you have the attitude of your onlookers to consider, and unless you know them to be sympathetic to your design, you had better conceal it. Women—though they deny it—generally feel hostile towards one of their own sex whom they see practising the arts of fascination, even when it involves no encroachment on their preserves. And men, as I have said, will give you no support when they perceive your cajoleries being spent elsewhere. Yet there is no need for you to lose altogether the advantage of talking to your prospective suitor about *himself,* the one topic which will certainly engross him and make him pleased with the person who broaches it. There is a way to manage it and still keep your motive entirely unsuspected.

SACCHARISSA What is it?

CYPRIA It is simply a matter of talking in "personalities" with everybody; then it will not be seen that you are singling him out from the rest.

SACCHARISSA Unless all present are my relations or intimate friends, I fail to understand how I can do this and retain any air of good breeding.

CYPRIA It needs a little ingenuity, but it can be done, and in such a manner as to increase rather than detract from your popularity. But perhaps an illustration is necessary to convey the kind of conversation that I mean. I once knew a lady who had a talent for reading—or seeming to read—palms.[2] It was the easiest of affairs to drop a hint of this accomplishment in any company, and soon all would be clamouring to hear something about themselves. So she would obligingly act the seer, and when she came to the man she liked, she would attribute to him only the characteristics which are, in the modern sense of the word, intriguing—the brave virtues and interesting faults. He would be flattered by her opinion, even if he were honest enough to know he did not deserve it; men are rare whose innate candour compels them to resist the enjoyment of a

■

[2] *I once knew a lady . . .*
Once just a party game, the seance took a more serious turn after the war, as grief-stricken survivors longed to communicate with the dead.

Palmistry does very well for a beginning if a man is inclined to be shy. It leads by gentle and almost imperceptible degrees to that most interesting of all subjects, himself, and to that tactful comment, dearest of all to the masculine heart; "You are not like other men!"   —Myrtle Reed, *The Spinster Book,* 1901 compliment because it is not true. Some of her statements, of course, would be sure to give rise to argument, and this would help her to exploit his egoism.

SACCHARISSA It really is a horrid idea. I am afraid I am too squeamish to put it into practice.

CYPRIA Many ordinary things sound horrid when described in plain terms to one who has never heard them treated so before. You have been exploiting people's egoism half your life without defining it. What is being "a good listener," for example, but the habit of appearing entertained while people talk about themselves, because you hope to be agreeable to them—in other words, to please their egoism, so as to make them well disposed towards you? Charm of manner itself, with whatever good intention, is surely a sort of exploitation of egoism. But I admit you should not call any of your little ruses by that name even to yourself. I, who have made it my task to give definitions, cannot avoid some bluntnesses.

SACCHARISSA Please tell me more about that guileful friend of yours. What else did she do?

CYPRIA When she had pleased and interested the man by her estimate of his character, she would look for the amatory indications. Her fingers might examine his hand with a somewhat caressing touch, but of course no one else could see that, and even he could not swear that it was deliberate! Then she would say very provocative things, but in such a way that the others who were present would think she was teasing him for their amusement; and she would adopt a slightly mysterious tone, as if she saw something she did not like to discuss before anyone else. She was generally successful, I believe, in engrossing men without being suspected of ulterior motives by the friends who introduced her to them.

SACCHARISSA Do you advise me to learn to read hands for the same purpose?

CYPRIA You may smile, Saccharissa, but fortune-telling, as long as the method is not too ridiculous, is to be numbered among the polite arts, whether it be taken seriously or not. Scarcely anything presents such opportunities for being personal in an impersonal fashion. Some games are very useful indeed, but you cannot seem so detached in them, and the occasions for playing them are comparatively rare.[3]

SACCHARISSA What games do you mean?

CYPRIA I was thinking of "Truth," in which you are supposed to answer all questions honestly or pay a forfeit, and "Percentages," which consists of giving people marks for their qualities, and inevitably leads to personal conversation. Nearly everyone consents with alacrity to play this kind of game, if the circumstances will admit of it. But, my dear, your question has occupied us so long that I had almost forgotten we must still discuss the method of approach with men whom you have known some time, as well as those whom you have not met at all.

SACCHARISSA I should like to hear how I can captivate a man whose acquaintance I have not made.

CYPRIA If he is associated with anyone you know, you will naturally manœuvre to have him introduced. You had better not ask for an introduction to be made, because it will

---

■

[3] *Some games are very useful indeed . . .*

This was the golden age of adult frivolity. Games like Charades, Dumcrambo, and Personalities belong to an era when hostesses were desperate to amuse guests at a "Saturday to Monday." Pleasure was organized into scheduled events. Contract bridge was a typical post-prandial activity, and those who couldn't play found themselves out of the social whirl.

Families often had their own private games, which they often forced upon unsuspecting guests.

probably reach his ears that you did so, thereby betraying your eagerness and preference in an ungraceful style. You may remember that I adjured you to be more flattering in words than in deeds. Seeking an introduction is a deed, and should only be done by stealth—that is, unless your position is so considerable that you can afford to play about with your prestige.

SACCHARISSA I think nearly every woman has enough self-respect to avoid the imputation of "running after" a man if she possibly can.

CYPRIA I call it not self-respect, but unconscious technique.

SACCHARISSA But tell me this, what am I to do when I long to meet a man who lives apart from my own world, and cannot be introduced to me either by request or manœuvring?

CYPRIA You must bear in mind the risk of the situation. To be seriously attracted by a stranger is to place your feet on ground that may prove solid, but is just as likely to crumble at every step. You are forming your favourable opinion upon superficialities alone. Be more than ever non-committal, therefore, in meeting a man who may prove totally unsuited to you. Make it seem, if you can, that he sought you out, not you him.[4]

SACCHARISSA Can this be done?

CYPRIA Yes, sometimes. At a dance, for instance,[5] and on several other occasions of pleasure, a smiling, genial glance will often cause the man at whom it is directed to make some advance to you. When you are sure of having created a pleasing impression, you can gradually assume a

■

[4] *Make it seem . . .*

In most mating rituals (and not only human ones), the female feigns passivity while subtly inviting the male to make his move. Timothy Perper, a biologist, and David Givens, an anthropologist, ventured into the wilds of the American singles scene to study the mating habits of the natives. After thousands of hours of observation, they concluded that women initiated fully two-thirds of all pick-ups in singles bars.

■

[5] *At a dance, for instance . . .*

Anthropologists, poets, and philosophers concur: Love usually begins with an interlocking of eyes. That initial intimacy with a stranger can be one of the most erotically charged moments in human experience. The Greeks believed that the exchange of glances between a man and a woman was a form of lovemaking in which the images of each other reflected in their eyes interpenetrated. John Donne draws upon this tradition in "The Exstasy," when the lover proclaims to his beloved: "Our eye-beams twisted, and did thread / Our eyes, upon one double string; / . . . And pictures in our eyes to get / Was all our propagation."

position which will dispel the memory of your tacit overture. Or if you can see in the first few minutes that he is
undesirable, your lack of responsiveness will soon send him
away, and he will probably consider he was mistaken in
imagining you had offered him any encouragement. But
many a woman is absurd enough to say something, perhaps
inadvertently, which lays her project bare and gives to a disagreeable man some shadow of justification for boasting
that she "flung herself at him."

SACCHARISSA Why did you refer expressly to occasions of pleasure? Did you mean that seductive smiles
would be out of place at other times?

CYPRIA If you smile at a stranger without the excuse of
high spirits and a propitious atmosphere, you will be very
much misunderstood.

SACCHARISSA If I were anxious to meet a man whom I
saw, say, in a train, an art gallery, or a hotel lounge, what
then?

CYPRIA Well, it is always conceivable that you may
require the loan of a pencil, or a match, or that you may need
to know the time or the way to somewhere, but you will
have to use such tactics as these with scrupulous care for
your dignity. Ask your question, whatever it may be, courte-
ously but in a perfectly business-like manner. Let all further
advances come from him, and if there are none, conceal the
least trace of mortification. If, on the other hand, he does
attempt conversation, be engaging but not over-responsive.
Should the acquaintance ripen into a flirtation, be on guard
against admitting any reason other than the ostensible one
for having addressed him in the first place.

SACCHARISSA In short, it would seem that in the love affair, as in other matters, you can do what you please so long as you are not found out.

CYPRIA I will not be so cynical as to endorse that statement. I merely warn you against wearing your heart on your sleeve.

SACCHARISSA I feel very well informed now upon your enticements for strangers, but I must ask you what course I am to take if I should suddenly decide to captivate an old friend.[6]

CYPRIA That is one of the pleasantest and most fruitful occupations I know, though it requires considerable time and patience. I might almost say that you have only to wish hard enough and your success is assured. You see, the case stands thus. If a man who obviously likes you has never made love to you, it is because from one cause or another he has never become aware of your physical attraction. But you must not believe that he cannot, therefore, ever be made aware of it. Perhaps his sexual attention was concentrated on someone else when he met you, perhaps for a similar reason you were not desirous of alluring him. What you have to do, then, is to bring your femininity to his notice by imperceptible degrees, and unless one grave obstacle impedes your progress, you should be able to achieve your purpose. Your task consists of being conscious of your sex during every moment that you spend with him. This consciousness will influence your speech, gesture, and bearing almost without your knowing it, and will convey to him by gradual stages a sense of your underlying charm—your quality of womanhood.

■

[6] *. . . I must ask you what course I am to take . . .*

Throughout *The Technique*, Cypria casually refers to friendships between the sexes—still a fairly radical notion. Any relationship that wasn't "going anywhere" (i.e., marriage) was considered a waste of time and a potential danger to a girl's reputation. Conventional wisdom held that the familiarity of friendship killed the possibility of romance.

"Darling, there's no such thing as friendship between an unmarried man and woman." Monica knew very well that from that Victorian stronghold her mother could never be moved.   —E. M. Delafield, *Thank Heaven Fasting,* 1932

SACCHARISSA You will not be surprised if I ask you what is the grave obstacle you have mentioned.

CYPRIA It is this. It may have happened that in the course of talks with this friend you have discussed the amorous emotions until you know too much about each other, and he would feel very self-conscious in doing with you the things he has spoken about. The more freely he has described his feelings, his methods and his foibles, the more he will shrink from letting you see them.

SACCHARISSA You think then that I could not make a truly intimate friend fall in love with me?

CYPRIA It would be difficult, but nothing is impossible to a patient and skilful woman. The disadvantage of your position would, at any rate, be nearly balanced by your superior opportunities for pursuing your design, and by the fact that, as you knew and liked him, you would not be liable to a painful disillusionment.

SACCHARISSA That femininity which you say I must assume is something I should like to hear more about.

CYPRIA You shall, if you will give me time to collect my thoughts. I have given you the bare framework of the principles of approach. It is for you to fill it out, and to adorn and embellish it according to your fancy. That is when your technique will come into its own, and distinguish you far above the women who have none.

Nine

...

She was the kind of woman men liked.
She amused them with her scatter-brain chatter
and innuendo and the fantasy she wove,
the stories she told, about herself. When she
was with women, she rested.

—ELIZABETH TAYLOR, "Oasis of Gaiety"
from *Hester Lilly,* 1954

CYPRIA I resume my pen to tell you about the conduct of a love affair. To that end I must treat of some aspects of your behaviour which I have not yet had occasion to mention, and expound more fully others to which I have only casually referred. You have asked for defined ideas upon femininity, and here you shall find them.

Men carry in their heads a great many ready-made notions on the characteristics of women, and in a general sense they are right. If you could analyse the minds of a dozen people of each sex,[1] you would doubtless find a very high percentage of the so-called feminine traits among the women, and a very low percentage among the men. But, of course, these traits are distributed in an irregular manner: a few women will have almost none, and a few will have almost all. And it does not need an especially acute perception to see that those who display numerous qualities of a proverbially feminine nature are more courted and beloved by men than those who seem masculine, or merely neutral. The more manly the man, the more womanly the woman who appeals to him.

Unless effeminate men delight you, it will be your endeavour to cultivate the characteristics which please the

■

[1] *If you could analyse the minds . . .*

For centuries the idea that men and women were fundamentally different was self-evident. Then in the 1970s, feminists argued that "feminine traits" were not intrinsic but the result of environmental conditioning in a patriarchal culture. Now, twenty-five years later, another generation is discovering that the opposite sex is indeed "the Other" and that certain traits *are* sex-specific. This idea has engendered an entire industry of books and seminars interpreting the behavior and habits of each sex to the other.

Moore's generation suffered from its own form of gender confusion. Many men returned from the front suffering from shell shock. Weepy, irrational, and emotional, they behaved like female hysterics. As women became more manly, men seemed further diminished. Nicholas Courtney cites a 1925 editorial in the *Daily Express* savaging the postwar male. "The Modern Girl's Brother" was "anemic, feminine, bloodless, dolled up like a girl, an exquisite without masculinity and resembling a silken-coated lap-dog." But not, the writer assured readers, homosexual.

■

2. . . . *in this matter as in others* . . .

The flapper heroine of Ursula Parrott's 1929 novel, *Ex-Wife,* casually remarks: "But I think chastity, really went out when birth control came in. If there is no consequence—it just isn't impor-tant. People's ideas—the things they say about *affaires*—begin to shift enormously, and their ideas are half a generation behind their conduct."

majority. From the books and plays men write, and the jokes they make, more even than from their attitude to yourself as an individual, you have probably discovered what they expect of women, and you may have observed that, in this matter as in others, fashions change.[2] In the middle days of the excellent Victoria, for instance, as in several earlier periods, women were placed on a most uncomfortable pedestal. They were generally regarded as ministering angels who spent all their time doing their duty: they were credited with immense potentialities for sacrific-ing themselves, and they were too delicate and romantically honourable for words. (This idealism, I need hardly say, had no room for the elderly. Very little seems to have been expected of them but nagging, prying, and gluttony.) Phys-ical purity and innocence were then highly fashionable. Without them a woman could have no status, and was more or less an outcast, pitied or despised. The sanctimonious morals of the Victorians were a reaction from the gal-lantries of their Regency parents, who had admired sophis-tication and whose society leaders were well known for their complicated intrigues; and that laxity was equally a reaction from the rigorous standards of what may be called the Johnsonian period, a time when everybody talked reli-gion and morality.

But although a man's taste will be swayed to a consider-able degree by the fashions of his time, inasmuch as they affect the prestige of the women with whom he associates, a certain fundamental principle of femininity exists, and may not be lightly set aside.

Its keynote is contrast. You know how the unsophisticated youth is enchanted by the glamour of the experienced, well-poised woman, while the jaded man of the world finds nothing really delectable but chastity; how a rugged, forceful man—though often joined through propinquity to a woman of his own type—is only fitted to mate with some soft, clinging creature who will lean upon him, and accept unquestioningly his protection and domination.

Carried beyond a certain point, however, contrast merely produces uncongeniality. You can appear different from the man who attracts you in a score of ways, and they will all enhance your prospect of winning him, if only each contrastive trait is one which he distinctly recognises as female. It would be of no use to be melancholy because a man is cheerful, or cheerful because he is melancholy, for those states of mind are not considered peculiar to our sex, and the contrast would be disagreeable rather than bewitching. Your differences must be such as perpetually indicate your womanhood. Let me set forth, therefore, the qualities, good and bad, which are regarded as especially our own.

The faults which are generally attributed to us in this epoch greatly outnumber our good points, and we hate them in each other, but I have noticed that men are very kind to most of them, despite an effort to grumble because they think they ought to. Now, as I enumerate our frailties, you might feel inclined to cry: "Oh no, you are wrong, I am not in the least like that!" So I will remind you in advance that because a fault is called feminine, that is not to say that every woman and no man may be accused of having it;

■

3 *They think us frivolous* . . .

These clichéd attributes, reflected in the epithets "scatter-brain," "busybody," "chatterbox," "cat," "bimbo," "spendthrift," and "gold digger," are personae invented by men but also frequently adopted by women to disguise their real power.

Apparently women act this way around men for a reason. In "Womanliness as a Masquerade" the psychiatrist Joan Rivière discusses this curious phenomenon: When in the company of men, competitive, accomplished women will suddenly turn girlish and wide-eyed. Is such behavior normal or pathological? To some extent, she concluded, almost all women adopt ultrafeminine poses to placate men and show that they pose no threat to their jobs, status, or masculinity. (Incidentally, Rivière was writing in the twenties.)

besides, I am telling you what all the world knows to be men's opinion of women, not necessarily my own.

They think us frivolous,[3] fond of chattering about trifles, and inclined to harp on one subject, especially if it does not concern us, disloyal and subtly hostile in our talk about one another, and not very good at keeping secrets. We are extravagant, they say, nearly insatiable in our passion for dress and pleasure, inconstant, capricious, and often selfish. They also consider us helpless and rather weak-minded, but as that is a feature they do not even pretend to grumble about, and as they so clearly dislike strong-minded women, I can no more call it a fault than I can put it down as a virtue.

As to virtues, alas, we are credited now-a-days with no more than two—two only which are still looked upon, in a vague way, as indigenous to the feminine composition; but they comprise a number of important features. They are refinement of taste, and tenderness of feeling.[4] After all that men have written about the perfidy and cruelty of women, in prose and verse, you would never be convinced that they applaud us for kindness of heart in our love affairs; but at least they admit that we frequently display an unselfish maternal devotion, that we are affectionate with children and animals, and shrink from the sight of suffering. "As gentle as a woman" is one of the very few common phrases about us which resemble a compliment.

I dare say you are surprised at this meagre catalogue of virtues, and perhaps you are wondering why I have omitted the domestic excellences for which we have been so highly praised in the past [*see* Fallen Angels *at the end of this chap-*

ter]. To speak truthfully, young men don't think about them or care a fig for them, except when they are brought daily to their attention by a mother, sister, or wife. Even if a man were habitually conscious of your domestic talent and goodness, that would not advance your amatory projects very far. He may like and respect the qualities he finds in his mother, but, despite the pathetic ballads sung in the music-halls, he will not become enamoured of them.

While we have youth and allurement, a man will be indulgent to them—will sometimes be amused and charmed with them, because they form a contrast to his own, and remind him quite excitingly of our different sex. (In exactly the same way, you know, we are rather charmed even by such unamiable characteristics of a man as his strange conservatism, and his stupid desire to knock down people who annoy him.) It is wise rather to display than conceal your feminine faults, so long as you make it perfectly apparent that they are only superficial, and that your integrity is uninjured by them. A man likes to look upon a woman as one who is subject to a hundred weaknesses and follies, and yet remains at heart a staunch friend, "a really good sort."

With this end in view, you will see that there are two or three habits on my list which should be eschewed. To begin with, it will not profit you to adopt the feline manner towards other women, however entertainingly you do it: ultimately, if not at first, your disloyalty will repel, and your palpable jealousy will suggest some conscious deficiency in yourself to one who might otherwise have seen none.

As for our babbling of secrets, it has long been tradi-

Whenever serious intellectuals—psychologists, sociologists, practicing physicians, Nobel Prize novelists—take time off from their normal pursuits to scrutinize and appraise the Modern American Woman they turn in unanimously dreary reports. They find her uninformed, intellectually lazy, lacking in ambition, and disgustingly docile in the presence of dominating males.

—Grace Adams,
Harper's, 1939

■

[4]. . . *tenderness of feeling.*

It seems that gender-specific traits such as "tenderness of feeling" are rooted in something deeper than custom. After observing and interviewing hundreds of adults and children of both sexes, the psychologist Carol Gilligan concluded that even in infancy females are more receptive to those around them. Later in life, women tend to define themselves in terms of their loyalties, obligations, and connections to others. Wired for motherhood, women are genetically—as well as culturally—predisposed to nurture.

■

[5] *The high-minded young woman of these days . . .*

Women's equality has done much to change men's views on the controversial question "Who pays?" In the 1950s, "Dutch Treat" spelled the kiss of death for romance. Beth Bailey cites an American "teen advisor" of the time: "If a boy lets you pay, he can't like you very much." Later, in the 1980s and 1990s, dating protocol grew more complicated. Many men, usually middle-class and college educated, admitted they preferred to pay, but they wanted their date to at least offer:

ADAM: *When I was in grad school, I dated a lawyer. I wouldn't have let her pay—ever—but knowing that I was spending gobs of money on tuition, I felt she should have at least offered.*

DAVID: *It dawned on me at some point that when women wouldn't let me pay, it's because they didn't want the expectation of . . . they didn't want the buyer-seller relationship, and I totally respected that.* —*Elle* magazine, roundtable discussion, 1995

tional, but on the whole I do not think we are less trustworthy than men [*see* On Gossip *at the end of this chapter*]. Our universal treachery, like other superstitions, is accepted without inquiry by a large number of men, but only affects the actions of the very credulous or those of singularly unfortunate experience. The average man, for all his timeworn gibes, does place his confidence in the women he likes, and could not withhold it if he would from those he loves. And perhaps, because we are more guileful than he is, we are also more discreet. We are not so easily taken unaware, being wily enough to detect the wiliness of others. Indeed, I am convinced that any woman worth considering is quite as fit to be the guardian of a man's confidence as he of hers. But, in the process of being trustworthy, do not become a strong, silent woman, do not lose your pretty, feminine loquacity. Chatter you must, because it is expected of you.

Extravagance and selfishness are the next matters which may deeply concern your integrity, and here I would like you to be particularly attentive to my counsel. There is a good deal of evidence in favour of the proposition that, unless a woman be somewhat exigent and luxurious, she is unlikely to be successful in her love affairs. The thrifty, industrious housewife is often amazed to learn that her husband, who never was generous to her, has lavished gifts upon some exacting siren. The high-minded young woman of these days,[5] who so carefully considers the pockets of her companions that she insists upon paying her own way, and sometimes theirs, will probably live to see them falling in love with others who are thoughtless and insouciant.

You see, the masculine mind is as vain as it is munificent. If it be not more than he can carry, a man enjoys the burden of providing for you, and he also enjoys the feeling that you are a dependent, *his* dependent, his creature. Take that away from him, and you take away an immense part of his delight in you. Though he may be as plastic as clay in your hands, he has *superficially* a wildly illogical desire to consider you his plaything,[6] an exquisite, elaborate toy, which requires very careful looking after, and is justifiably expensive. He may complain loudly about the high cost of women, but there are some protests which have more the nature of a boast than of an honest desire to be rid of an affliction. If, from whatever praiseworthy motive, you refuse to fulfil a function with which he has invested you—in this case, the absurd but pleasant pretence of being a plaything—you are relinquishing one of the distinctions between your sex and his which embody your whole charm for him.

Only when your attractions are exceedingly numerous can you preserve your financial independence without jeopardising your power; when an ordinary woman does so, she may form a friendship, but she will not gain a lover.

Your best practice is to be as dependent materially as you are independent spiritually. As I have said more than once, you must not seem spiritually to find him a necessity, but materially each new symptom of your reliance on him will constitute a new endearment—that is, I need hardly say, when you are certain of your favourable reception. Nor must you commit the grave error of taste which accepts entertainments or presents as if they were to be taken for

There's an uneasy association between the legitimate date, in which a man pays for a woman's company, and a tryst with a prostitute, in which he pays for her sexual favors. Before the term "date" became common usage in America, it was prostitutes' slang for an appointment with a paying customer. Indeed, prostitutes still approach men with the query, "Are you looking for a date?"

If the man is courting, he pays—and a woman almost instinctively knows her partner is wooing her. In fact, there is no more widespread courtship ploy than offering food in hopes of gaining sexual favors in exchange.
—Helen K. Fisher, *Anatomy of Love,* 1992

[6] *. . . he has* superficially *a wildly illogical desire . . .*

At one time or another, even the most enlightened man yearns to see his wife or girlfriend as a child, a frivolous creature to cherish and indulge. She could be an executive with a salary double his own, a rocket scientist with twice his IQ, but he'll find some area in which he's superior. A small chink in the armor is disarming. Denis Thatcher, the retiring husband to the former British prime minister known as the Iron Lady, once recalled, "She stood for Dartford twice and lost twice, and the second time she cried on my shoulder I married her."

Cypria doesn't advise a woman to *be* an extravagant toy, but to temporarily *pretend* she is. In its early stages, a love affair is a game in which each participant assumes the part most likely to draw the other into deeper involvement. More often than not, lovers pretend to be something they're not. Some women find the role titillating, a diversion from workaday life. Besides, by its very nature, romantic love is a form of regression. Lovers indulge in baby talk, teasing, pet names, and private games. As Freud noted, "Man becomes childish when in love." Woman too.

■

[7] *You are pictured by men . . .*

The feminine delight in baubles and trinkets is deeply imbedded in popular culture—and in the male psyche: "Give me, buy me, take me" is the mantra of the modern Lorelei. In the 1930s, Jean Harlow, incandescent in white satin, sprawled on silken sheets, popping bonbons; in the 1950s and 1960s, a

granted. Your gratitude must never cease to be graceful and enthusiastic while you wish him to love you.

You do not gather, I trust, that I would counsel you to lead anyone into prodigal and ostentatious display. That would scarcely be compatible with integrity, and is exactly what I would warn you not to do. Within reason, however, you should allow him to be generous to you, and indeed, if he does not try to show some generosity according to his means, I should not think him attached to you with any but a very trivial kind of partiality [*see* Gifts *at the end of this chapter*].

You are pictured by men as a being with an eternal hunger for unaccountable numbers of clothes, trinkets, perfumes, chocolates, and posies, and your correct technique is to appear so.[7] He will take a pleasure in supplying you with objects of luxury which he would not buy for himself, and he will consider it feminine in you to accept them at his hands, or even to coax him for them. Be sure, however, that until you have won him, you take from him only objects of luxury, and not those that are necessary to your existence.[8] This is a strange statement, but I will try to explain myself.

It is true I have said that the more you rely upon a man the more you will endear yourself. But it is not consistent with the state of being a charming, elegant toy with whom he seeks distraction from worries, that you should have worries of your own, excepting those very little ones that provoke a smile rather than sympathetic dejection. When you make a man aware that you are needy, and accept from him such things as meet irrefutably real requirements, he cannot think of you any longer as a pretty plaything; you have become a serious person with serious cares of the sort he knows himself, a member of his own troubled world.

One class of men is exempt from this rule, namely, those who are so superlatively rich as never to have experienced the slightest monetary difficulty. For them you do not lose your air of unreality by sharing in the common struggle, for the simple reason that the struggle is not common and is hardly credible to those who never have taken part in it. You would have a more interesting unreality to this kind of man in being frankly at a loss to make ends meet, if that is your plight, than in attempting to keep up with the women of his own circle, whose magnificence has no novelty for him. But even from a very wealthy man, dearest Saccharissa, you should not take a direct gift or loan of money unless your position with him be a perfectly secure one. Most men have a crude association of ideas in connection with giving money to a woman, which would be likely to influence their attitude towards you quite without their knowing it themselves.

Of course you cannot remain for ever the pretty plaything. In the tide of time a man must grow to see you more or less as you are. If you meet him often and intimately, countless small factors will join to strip you of glamour, but do not, by excess of candour, shed it yourself at the beginning of the relationship. You cannot afford to dispense with artificial charm until you have gained some hold, and even then you must not do anything distinctly disenchanting; but little by little, and not too seriously, you should lift your

mink stole was the *summum bonum* of every woman's existence, whether showgirl or society matron, and in the 1980s, Madonna's "material girl" sang, "Only boys who save their pennies can make my rainy day." Finally, in 1995, *Cosmopolitan* continues the tradition with a cover story designed to make any man cringe: "How to Marry a Billionaire," a title that sounds like a 1950s romantic comedy, adjusted for inflation.

A kiss on the hand might feel very good, but a diamond tiara is forever.
—Lorelei Lee in
Gentlemen Prefer Blondes, 1953

∎

[8]*Be sure, however . . .*

The wooer arrives, bearing chocolates, flowers, and perfume, luxuries that entice the senses and quicken desire. In *A Natural History of Love* (1994) Diane Ackerman notes that the classic offerings of courtship are associated with sex: Flowers are a plant's reproductive organs; chocolate is a mild stimulant similar to the chemical we emit when in the throes of passion (it was also reputed to be an aphrodisiac); and many perfumes contain musk or civet, the effluvia emitted by the civet cat in heat. On the other hand, such practical gifts as, say, Tupperware would be an unpleasant intrusion of the real world into the lovers' rarefied atmosphere.

■

[9] *One of our best methods of flattering a man . . .*

As a typical male teenager declared in a 1949 *Ladies' Home Journal* article, "I don't mind if a girl knows more than I do. . . . I just like her to act like she knows a little less."

In Japan, traditional feminine behavior has been ritualized. When in the presence of a man, an educated Japanese woman might lapse into an idiom known as *huriko,* a giggly, sing-song chatter designed to propitiate men by making them feel superior and protective.

Two decades after the publication of *The Technique of the Love Affair,* in *The Vulgar Heart,* Moore wrote of gender roles and how they divert and discomfort and enchant each sex: "That one sex consists of yearning, clinging, and devoted creatures is a conception flattering to the other and therefore not readily to be relinquished

spangled, trifling mask, and show the true face beneath, or else you will never have a chance of revealing the deeper qualities which a man does, in some paradoxical way, hope for in a woman who strongly attracts him. You can captivate easily enough without those qualities, as I have said, but sustaining admiration for an indefinite period is another matter.

When I tell you that you must eventually give indications of what is called "better nature," do not imagine that there is any stage in a love affair at which you can show yourself as completely unselfish, and ready to immolate all your own fancies and ambitions upon the altar of your devotion. No such time ever comes; but you can display good nature, a sense of honour, and a capacity for friendship, without going to disconcerting extremes.

Now a word, Saccharissa, on helplessness. One of our best methods of flattering a man is to pretend that we are perfectly idiotic in every matter in which he is accomplished,[9] except when to be similarly accomplished would mean an especial congeniality and increase your opportunities of meeting him, as in games and sports and arts, for example. If you are, say, a very good tennis player and you seek to beguile someone who is himself an expert in this game, your skill will be an excellent asset, provided that you do not eclipse him or try to instruct him, *particularly in the presence of others.* But, in general, contrast is desirable, and even in the few matters I have mentioned you must rarely let your skill exceed his.

A man falls in love with a woman who helps him to

appear at his best. Many women have no realisation of this, and earnestly compete with the man they wish to fascinate, struggling to win arguments, pointing out his shortcomings to him, and often holding him up to ridicule.

You must be sure to be inefficient in most of the things wherein he is practical. If he is the sort of man who invariably remembers to label luggage, file receipts, and apply for dog licences, you must allow yourself to be vague and silly on every subject of the kind. If, on the contrary, he is one of the rarer type, the dreamers, you will command his wondering admiration by efficiency.

There is but one branch of affairs in which you can always show capability, with whomever you concern yourself, and yet not detract from your femininity; that is, in anything which touches your much-praised tenderness of feeling. "When pain and anguish wring the brow,"[10] a man still likes to be able to call you a ministering angel, just as at other times he still enjoys your being uncertain, coy, and hard to please. In the more sombre of his daydreams, the woman he loves flits about his sick-bed—light, gentle, and more useful than half-a-dozen nurses—or, with her hand in his, kneels beside the chair in which he sits, bowed down with strife or sorrow. You cannot be too helpful in such cases as these, Saccharissa.

Before I close a chapter which is too short for my purpose but too long, I fear, for your pleasure, I must devote a moment to the one other creditable feature which men definitely expect to find in us—refinement of taste. It does not sound like much of a virtue, unless you recollect that it

by them: many women, to give men what they are said to want, pretend to feminine weakness from which they secretly derive amusement. Men likewise are known to emphasize their so-called masculine traits in the presence of women, sometimes assuming pugnacity, sexual vigour, and the will to dominate beyond the degree that comes naturally to them."

■

[10] *"When pain and anguish wring the brow"*. . .

Are women better caretakers than men or is this just a role ingrained from centuries of habit? One generation unwittingly provided an experiment. The women's movement of the 1970s produced a quiet revolution among educated, middle-class men. Encouraged to share their feelings and to weep, men were told that they too could be "caring" and emotive. Some assumed traditionally female roles and occupations such as nursing and homemaking. With machismo passé, these men were forced to alter their seduction tactics: They wooed with slim volumes of Sylvia Plath and "shared" feelings. They downplayed rather than displayed their masculinity. Yet despite their feminist convictions, some women were unable to reverse centuries of conditioning: All too often the new man found himself thrown over for an insensitive jerk.

includes a vital trinity: delicacy of mind, speech, and person. You would be astonished if you knew how many women seek to prove themselves modern by the use of indelicate conversation and coarse language. I cannot too emphatically condemn a manner which does so much harm to all our sex. If men cease to believe that we are beings of a finer fibre than themselves, where will be the chivalry which we require of them, and which is certainly our due? There are some, I know, who will tolerate this coarseness in a woman, and a few depraved palates that relish it; but, even when it does not injure her own prospect of attracting, respect for the rest of her sex should restrain her verbal abandon.

Feminine conversation should be absolutely free from all revolting elements, and a man should be conscious that there is a very decided difference between the topics upon which he can talk with you and those reserved for the ears of his own sex [see On Feminine Conversation at the end of this chapter]. If he does not feel this, you will gather that he has consorted with misleading types of women, and you will correct his impression as rapidly as you can. Always avoid all words and phrases which in themselves conjure up a disagreeable picture, and do not indulge in long discussions of morbid or sordid matters. As for stories of a bawdy kind, a man who attempts to tell you one of those on short acquaintance is insulting you, unintentionally or otherwise. Many women, lacking the moral courage to rebuke the offender with icy silence, summon up a laugh to gratify him.

Of the essential features of personal delicacy, you naturally have nothing to learn. Yet there are one or two other facets of the subject which should be examined. They may properly be placed in the next chapter, and there I shall make haste to deal with them.

Fallen Angels

. . . perhaps you are wondering . . . (p. 134)

Nowhere is the birth of the modern woman more obvious than in Cypria's cursory dismissal of the domestic arts, hitherto a woman's chief glory. Before labor-saving devices and bachelor flats, skills such as preserving, sewing, and cooking increased a woman's value on the marriage market. The unsung housewife attained her apotheosis during the Victorian age. Coventry Patmore's "The Angel in the House," an interminable paean to married love and family values, was a best seller of its age and a risible cliché thereafter. The poem seems more like a mock heroic, as Patmore endows bourgeois minutiae with unexpected gravity: "Dear Saint, I'm still at High-Hurst Park. / The house is filled with folks of mark." Or, "Our witnesses the cook and groom, / We signed the lease for seven years more." Except for its title, which has become a catch phrase for the Victorian ideal of womanhood, the poem is virtually forgotten. Perhaps, as Morton Hunt points out, even Patmore found his own household angel forgettable. After her death, he duly recorded in his diary:

> Remember above all, the 5,410 days she was my wife, and on each one of which, though nothing happened to be remembered, she did her duty to me, her children, her neighbours, and to God, with a lovely unnoticeable evenness and completeness.

By the 1920s, the angel had become a frump in a housecoat and domestic skills had been brushed aside for more tantalizing ones.

...

On Gossip

As for our babbling . . . (p. 136)
In *Gossip* (1985), Patricia Meyer Spacks defends "idle" chatter and explores its historical identification with women: "For centuries, commentators have pointed out that men gossip too: combating the folk myth that gossip belongs mainly to women. No one ever says that women gossip *too*." Tale-telling is frivolous and unmanly, an

activity for those with too much time on their hands. Men exchange information, women tattle; men are strong and silent, women are weak-minded and loquacious. At the risk of irritating those around her, a woman can proclaim her femaleness merely by chattering foolishly.

From pulpits and in pamphlets, men have inveighed against the female tendency to prattle. A garrulous wife was a danger to her husband, a betrayal of his secrets the verbal equivalent to adultery. A loose tongue could destroy marriages, careers, social position, and most important, one's reputation. Christian moralists implied that the ills of the world could be traced to one woman who didn't know when to stop talking: Eve, who, as Spacks points out, "brought sin into the world by unwise speaking and unwise listening." Women have a vested interest in personal talk. Tabloids aside, gossip usually consists of a small group talking about those who are not present; it is domestic and private, its stock in trade the intimate life of its subjects. Men are seemingly less interested in the interior self and in private relationships—yet even they recognize the value of gossip in the larger world. A Washington politician told Spacks that while *he* never gossiped, his wife did, and he depended on her to relay anything he needed to know. (His wife vehemently denied this.)

Another reason for women's association with gossip is that, paradoxically, talk is the only weapon for those who have no voice. Wives often talk about their husbands the way servants gossip about their employers, ridiculing them, analyzing their habits, betraying their dirty little secrets. Spacks calls such talk "an outlet for the subordinate."

■ ■ ■

Gifts

Within reason, however, you should allow him . . . (p. 138) In every culture and in every period in human history the exchange of gifts from male to female is integral to the courtship process. In primitive societies a wooer left a piece of fresh meat at a woman's dwelling; in the Western world, men send flowers or provide dinner at an expensive restaurant. Women have traditionally been the passive recipients of male largesse, and both sexes unquestioningly accept their roles in the exchange. If a woman showers her beau with gifts and pays his way, she reverses the established balance of power—and society tends to view the relationship with suspicion.

Whether viewed as a love token or a bribe, a gift serves various purposes in the mating dance. It can be a lure to catch a reluctant mistress, a flashy display of virility, or proof that he's a "good provider." According to the anthropologist Mary Batten, females of various species judge the wooing male by the size of his gift. The female scorpion fly, for instance, rejects any offering under a minimum size.

Sometimes a present signals the degree of a man's intentions, its worth being in proportion to the donor's seriousness and urgency. If read correctly, it conveys nuances of feeling from mild esteem to uncontrollable ardor, from flickering interest to the end of the affair. Knowing this, women try to interpret a gift's "meaning." The recipient eagerly examines the object, reading it as if it were the Rosetta stone; she discusses it with friends, often investing it with a significance far beyond the suitor's imagination. Often she's wrong. The nonsmoking woman who received a cigarette lighter from her boyfriend gave up the relationship for lost, yet two months later he proposed. Another received the sound track to *Sleepless in Seattle* and was sure she was unforgettable, but it turned out he was moving to Seattle without her.

In an attempt to share their deepest selves, serious lovers exchange personal objects: servicemen give dog tags, students present fraternity rings, sweaters, or favorite books. The Jane Austen devotee who reads a Tom Clancy novel reads with her beloved's eyes, and thus bridges the gap between them.

To the modern woman this advice seems dated, yet in 1996—about seventy-five years after *The Technique*—the female authors of a hugely popular dating manual insist their readers sever relations with a man if he fails to produce lavish gifts on Valentine's Day and her birthday. Yet even the most sensible woman usually cares more about gifts (and cards, flowers, and so on) than the average man. In the feminine eye, a present is affection made tangible. Perhaps there's some truth to the chestnut about the husband who perpetually forgets his anniversary—much to his wife's annoyance. But all gifts, whether cheap or dear, show that a man is thinking about the recipient in her absence—a crucial step in the development of a love affair.

■ ■ ■

On Feminine Conversation

Feminine conversation . . . (p. 142)
A generation earlier, Cypria's warning would have been unnecessary and unthinkable. Victorian gentlemen quietly withdrew after dinner to the smoking room, where they would discuss politics or swap bawdy

stories. Language, no less than dress, distinguished the sexes. Women were excluded from conversation that was complicated, suggestive, or unpleasant. Thus Lord Brougham was outraged when the commission on child labor published its findings—but not out of compassion for chimney sweeps. He was disturbed by its potential effect on women and "young persons." Married women were allowed more liberties than the unmarried, who were considered especially vulnerable and childlike. A true lady remained silent.

Virginia Woolf recalled the precise moment that she and her sister, Vanessa, were liberated from the stifling proprieties of speech. One spring evening in 1908, Lytton Stratchey, noticing a stain on her skirt, mischeviously asked, "Semen?" With that word, Woolf wrote, "all barriers of reticence and reserve went down." Bohemian Bloomsbury could debate abstruse issues and casually drop words like "bugger" and "copulation" in mixed company, but it took another generation and a world war to break down the verbal barricade between ordinary men and women.

In wartime such coyness came to seem quaint, even grotesque. Women who nursed soldiers or listened to their husband's stories unconsciously began to pick up their idioms, slang, and curses. The phrases and images of an ugly war began infiltrating the drawing rooms of civilized men and women.

But true linguistic equality did not arrive until the sexual revolution of the 1960s and the women's movement of the 1970s. After centuries of suppression, liberated women seized the "F word" like starving peasants given bread.

Today, for better or worse, we have partially returned to the old divisions: Some colleges have adopted speech codes prohibiting the use of certain words in front of women, and men who verbally offend women often find themselves slapped with a lawsuit for sexual harassment.

Ten

■ ■ ■

In a country where there aren't enough men
to go around girls have got to take trouble
if they want lives of their own.

—E. M. DELAFIELD,
Thank Heaven Fasting, 1932

CYPRIA   The questions of delicacy and taste which we have still to discuss are those which most men will swear they do not care about.

"Why do you put that stuff on your face?" a man will say to a woman, as he watches her employing powder and lip-rouge; "I'd like you much better without it" [*see* Cosmetics *at the end of this chapter*]. And so he honestly believes. But if, in the hope of increasing his regard, she allowed him to see her with the shiny face and pink lips which are so much commoner in reality than our proverbial "milk and roses," she would be sadly disillusioned in her effect upon him. When he criticises her cosmetics, it is because, never having seen her entirely without them, he chivalrously imagines that she does not need them. Why should she undeceive him of this charming belief?

In any case, no ordinary modern man is truly repelled by our aids and accessories to beauty, though he may try hard enough to object to them on principle—the old-fashioned principle that Nature should be left to her own devices. By pointing the contrast between our habits and his, they actually form a blandishment. You will not conceive, I trust, that I am referring to heavy make-up, which, by rendering you conspicuous, would prove a grave error. No, your

The "sex goddesses" of the age—
Dietrich, Harlow, and Garbo—
possessed a glamour that was
defiantly artificial and exaggerated. Features were unabashedly
plucked, pulled, painted, and
straightened. In *Sunset Boulevard*
the aging star Norma Desmond
sighs for the era when women,
"had faces"; for her generation,
the real face was the mask one
presented to the world.

*[Jane] found herself quite unable to
look at Prudence, whose eyelids were
startlingly and embarrassingly
green, glistening with some greasy
preparation which had little flecks of
silver in it. Was this what one had to
do nowadays when one was unmarried? she wondered. What hard work
it must be. . . . The odd and rather
irritating thing about it was, though,
that Nicholas was gazing at Prudence with admiration; it was quite
noticeable. So it really did work.*
                —Barbara Pym,
          Jane and Prudence, 1953

■

[1] *Because he thinks he ought to
like* . . .
    A prominent marriage coun-
selor, writing in the late 1940s,
echoed this sentiment, citing—of
all things—a survey of potential

appearance should never seem to have required more artificial aid than the majority of other women use, even though
it may really have done so.

Even when a man has taken you under his wing for ever
and you feel that you possess him, you should still attempt
to indulge yourself in the little trinkets and small trifles of
finery which so excite his wonder and amusement. If, from
consideration for his purse, for instance, you never were to
expose a craving for all these vanities, he would begin to
suspect something lacking in your femininity, and would be
dimly dissatisfied.

All through a love affair you are in danger of believing
what the average man tells you about his taste in women,
and modelling yourself upon it, when it is really the very
reverse of what he feels. Because he thinks he ought to like
this and dislike that, he will frequently convince himself
that he positively does so.[1] But you must not believe him
simply because he believes himself.

For example, his code of ethics keeps reminding him that
he ought not to fall in love with a woman merely because
she is pretty, and soft, and scented, and exquisitely attired,
and flattering; and that it would be nobler of him to succumb only to goodness, and common-sense, and domesticity. So he tells you that looks are nothing to him, and that
what he likes is character. "You needn't bother to dress up
for me," he says, "I should like you just as well without a
spot of powder on your face, pottering round the house in
an old gingham apron." And so he would once in a while if
your apron were rather picturesque, and you didn't take
him literally about the powder. The intimacy of your aspect

would enchant him while it remained a novelty, but you could not afford to dispense too often with your frivolities. Likewise, he does not care to confess, either to himself or to you, the hunger for approbation which makes your flattery so delicious, and he informs you that he hates being flattered, that he can bear the truth about himself, and would rather hear it candidly spoken than be paid a dozen glossy compliments. Yet how long would he pursue you if you always talked to him in terms of plain, unvarnished truth?

Be cautious, then—be doubly, doubly cautious, Saccharissa, that you do not commit tactical errors because he tells you, even with passionate sincerity, that they will raise you in his esteem.

I have heard of a man who was unconsciously clever enough to launch his love affair with the following precaution, cunningly expressed to the object of his tenderness: "I hope that you will never act the coquette with me, my dearest girl. I am the sort of man who responds only to kindness and love, and the more that you yield to me and love me, the more constant I shall be to you. So do not think that by withholding yourself from me you will be making me more ardent. Now promise me, promise me, dearest, that you will be perfectly natural with me, and will never resort to any coquetries as far as I am concerned!"

The credulous girl immediately promised, and was amazed to find that continued yielding and manifestations of love on her part satiated him just as rapidly as if he had been the most inferior of mankind: she learned to regret indeed that she had forsworn her coquetries.

Men are like unruly children clamouring for enough

car buyers taken by Chrysler Corporation after World War II. Most of them said they wanted a car that was economical, practical, and easy to park, and that appearance was inconsequential. Chrysler produced a modest-looking, smaller Plymouth. The model bombed. At the same time, General Motors introduced a powerful, flashy, gas-guzzling Buick. It sold well. The conclusion of car manufacturers (and marriage counselors): People will tell you what they think they *should* like, not what they really want.

sweets all at once to make them ill. The wise nurse gives one sweet at a time; so also the wise lover. But, of course, there are special occasions! On some days rewards must be granted. Be careful that these times of utter complaisance come only when every circumstance is propitious, and nothing from without or within will arise to mar the hour. For this reason a yielding, either physical or spiritual, should rarely be spontaneous. Impromptus are seldom perfect: Besides, you should not deprive a fellow creature of the pleasures of anticipation.

A sense of the fitness of things may not for an instant be dispensed with in the amorous art. Attention is ensnared by looks or fame or any other kind of prestige, but it cannot be retained save by a woman who knows *the right moment* for everything—and the right moment is rarely the one that a man attempts to press upon her. She who never gives herself until she can do so in the correct setting, the perfect atmosphere, and at the zenith of her power; who never seeks to excite passion in a man who is tired or disturbed, or asks him if he loves her save when she knows that he is longing for the opportunity of saying so; who realises exactly when to call for a sacrifice, inflict a punishment, confess a wrong-doing, express a misgiving—she, once having obtained her admirer, will be invincible.

Let us very briefly investigate the errors to which I have just referred, and a few others that are commonly practised by women in love affairs. First, there is the folly of allowing yourself to be won without adequate preparation, taken unaware. I don't mean that the man has not known you and perhaps made love to you for some time, but that the occasion of your surrender was not prearranged and is lacking in the ideal background. Though he may have pursued you unavailingly for weeks or months beforehand, the sudden complete crumbling of your fortress will make him think that its walls were not, after all, so strong as he imagined; and, forgetting his previous failures, he will consider his victory an easy one. What he wins, or thinks he wins, easily, he will not esteem. Your fortress, whatever it guards—your virtue, your freedom, your passion, or your love—should crumble very slowly and reluctantly. But when at last you do grant him a victory, let it be a pleasant one! Let your surrender be thrilling or even amusing, but do not let it be pathetic.

Some women are constantly afflicted with remorse for what, by their own free will, they have conceded, and thus irritate or depress the man who should be proudly delighting in his (purely nominal) conquest. The wife, for example, who is always lamenting the lost independence of her single days, provokes the fondest husband to remind her eventually that she married him from choice. And as he thinks out retorts of this kind, his affection begins to be undermined. The citadel should fall slowly, as I say, but within he should find feasting and revelry, not wailing and gnashing of teeth.

Another solecism is the attempt to arouse a fatigued or worried man to demonstrations of emotion. Many of us are insatiable in our longing for the outward signs and words of love,[2] or else we are perverse, and want a man only when we see that he does not want us. It is not very difficult for a woman to have her way in this as in almost any other mat-

■

[2]*Many of us are insatiable . . .*

It is proverbial that after a woman tells a man she loves him, he assumes she'll continue to do so until she says otherwise. In contrast, women seem to require periodic updates on a man's emotional temperature. Fear and anxiety, and the behavior they engender, are lethal to love and well-being. In *Pleasure, A Discursive Guide-Book,* Moore writes:

The climate of sexual emotion is tropical, and in it anxieties as well as pleasures grow with a wild luxuriance. . . .

Then we ask, "Do you love me?" "Do you love me as much as you did last year?" "Will you love me next year?" "Were you faithful to me last month?" "What are your inmost thoughts about me . . . ?"

I think there is no allurement so potent, physically and mentally as reposefulness, a charm even more seductive than vitality. . . .

ter, if she is persistent enough; but it is a poor sort of triumph to have teased expressions of devotion from a man
whose brain is fixed on other topics, or to have awakened
unwilling passion. By taking the rôle of suppliant (which
you should leave to him in everything but requests for
material possessions and enjoyments), you make him feel
that the right order of things has been upset, and give him a
mortifying memory of yourself.

Your task is to create a love affair as free as possible from
any association of ideas that could embarrass. You know, it
is a good thing to make a man angry with you sometimes,
but it is always a bad thing to embarrass him.

Do not expect your admirer to be for ever stating his
feelings in so many words, unless he happens to specialise
in them; but, on the other hand, you must be wary with a
man who never commits himself. If he loved you, or imagined he loved you, he would tell you so at least once in the
course of his overtures. Before he has revealed his state of
mind soberly and succinctly, make no concessions of any
importance, but once he has done so, it is very unwise to
demand repetitions and confirmations, for it will seem to
indicate over-anxiety. Besides, even the most patient and
affectionate people get tired of being asked the same question an unlimited number of times, and when a man's
tongue begins to weary of protesting his admiration, his
spirit will weary too.

Another error of judgment made by an unskilled woman
is the practice of calling attention to her own defects, which
would, perhaps, otherwise pass unnoticed. A flaw which
can be concealed should be concealed; if this is not possible,

the woman should make no apology for it, and the man, through always ignoring the imperfection out of politeness, will very probably forget its existence. Of course, I am not speaking of real afflictions or abnormalities, but only the ordinary deficiencies of which we nearly all have a good many.

I once watched a woman hold up her hand to a man whom she wished to attract, and exclaim laughingly: "Look what hideous finger-nails I have! My hands are really so dreadful that I'm quite ashamed of them—so coarse and red. I can't do anything with them!" He murmured something to assure her they were not so bad as she thought, but she had definitely planted in his mind the knowledge that her hands were very ugly, and though that one feature by itself would not have been enough to cause dissatisfaction, a few more such candid moments must have resulted in a most unnecessary depreciation of his opinion. If she had not herself exposed her weak points, he might still have noticed them, but they would have appeared without stress, and left only a light impression.

Another example may be found in the common case of the woman who is a few years older than the man she cherishes, and who needlessly reminds him of the fact by such incessant harpings on the theme of his youth that he begins to think of her in terms of great age.

Eschew every mistake of this kind, but if it should happen that you see a man's attention focused on one of your imperfections, either by his own volition or through the tactlessness or malice of another person, do not pretend to be unconscious of it. A flaw which you seem not to have

■

[3] *Never be led away . . .*

Cypria's advice is as valid today as it was seventy years ago. Upon first encounters, some modern women might disclose a sordid history of sexual abuse or eating disorders or might casually mention that they hate their boss. The size of the problem is immaterial—it's just that there *is* one. An abundance of complexes—"baggage"—is certain to drive most men away. (Paradoxically, a man can enjoy caring for and protecting a woman—as long as her problems are small, manageable, or intriguing.)

According to the linguist Deborah Tannen, each sex responds differently to exchanges of confidences. Women welcome intimate talk, seeing it as a way to establish a bond. Men interpret "trouble talk"—to use Tannen's expression—as a plea for help, an obligation to solve a problem. Whether justified or not, they perceive her as a potential nuisance.

observed in yourself makes you look ridiculous. You know how people are made fun of who are ignorant of their own shortcomings. You should show a sense of yours whenever it is desirable to do so, but at all other times an attitude of self-complacency is the only one that you should cultivate.

For the successful practice of most arts, although a certain confidence in one's powers is necessary in private, one must generally adopt a modest public manner. The love affair is different: You must display your assurance and conceal your humility.

Never be led away to pour into the ears of a man whom you would capture,[3] confidences that will totally destroy your prestige, such as that you are lonely, have few friends and no other admirers, and would miss him painfully if you were not to see him, and so forth. I have touched upon this subject before, and I recall it to you now because it is very vital. He should always believe that you could replace him, if you wished, with consummate ease. Even your husband should carry this article of faith for ever in the recesses of his mind, so that when you are a grey old woman he will be still able to declare: "Ah, Saccharissa might have had her choice of a dozen different men! I wonder what she saw in me."

When you part from him (I have gone back to his bachelor state now), you should nearly always leave to him the matter of proposing your next meeting. You may recollect that when I told you to be generous with appreciation, and to spare no kindness that your tongue could frame, I made an exception of flatteries, which though they might give him some pleasure, would tend to lower your standing in his eyes. In this category comes the mistake of being the first to suggest another meeting. "When shall I see you again?" is a flattering question[4]—from you a far too flattering question. Keep it for reward-days.

Agreeable partings are more important than agreeable meetings, for a bad effect on meeting can be dispelled before you leave each other, but a bad effect on parting makes an impression that remains until you see each other again.

Be especially careful that any unpleasant atmosphere which may have pervaded the moments just spent together has quite lifted by the time one of you has to go elsewhere. I am not warning you now against angry partings. An angry atmosphere is one thing, an unpleasant atmosphere is another. It is sometimes not a bad policy to let him go away in a temper, or to be in a temper yourself; a love affair made of sugar throughout would soon cloy. But unpleasant atmospheres, according to my interpretation, are the less healthy exhalations of something amiss between you which has not been brought into the light of day. Have you never known one of those dreary meetings, Saccharissa, when you felt convinced that he was—not furious with you, or jealous of you, or anything stimulating like that, but simply not enjoying you? Those are the hours that, unskilfully managed, can demolish amorous emotion more surely than the angriest quarrels or the fiercest jealousies.

It is generally some incident too small for explanation which gives rise to his nameless antagonism. Or perhaps he is in an irritable mood when he comes to meet you, and your manner in the first few minutes unwittingly jars

■

[4] *"When shall I see you again?"*...
By 1920 courtship had changed: In an earlier time, a woman could ask any socially acceptable man to call on her. She appointed times for his arrival and departure, and few gentlemen dared overstep the limits.

"I've got no one but you now," she murmured in a melting voice.
She fancied in her ignorance that the expression of this sentiment would please him. She was not aware that a man is usually rather chilled by it, because it proves to him that the other is thinking about his responsibilities and not about his privileges.
—Arnold Bennett,
The Old Wives Tale, 1908

In Bennett's fictional exchange, the woman sees her avowal as an expression of love and trust, whereas to her lover it signifies a "chilling" dependency that will prove burdensome. Women on the verge of a relationship—or a nervous breakdown—should reserve private disclosures for other women.

instead of soothes him. Perhaps—if the affair be still in its early days—you seem less attractive this time than he has thought you on previous occasions, and he is uncomfortable because he has a vague idea that he no longer wants to pursue you, and yet doesn't know how to draw back without hurting your feelings. If you suspect this to be his mental condition, you will probably grow depressed and lose yet more attraction in his eyes as you do so; but there is no reason for you to take his coldness to heart. It is more often than not an absolutely natural reaction from having been too much entranced. You will find it far better ultimately that he undergoes two or three comparatively small reactions in the initial stages than that there should be one enormous recoiling of his senses after long infatuation.

Of course, it requires craftsmanship to tide him over one of these listless, or disappointed, or faintly hostile moods, so that he has practically forgotten what it was all about by the time he sees you again. Low spirits are infectious, and you will have some difficulty in keeping up yours while they are in contact with his. Gaiety, charm, and a little teasing—so long as they do not seem laboured—may change his frame of mind before he leaves you: if  they do not clear the atmosphere, you are permitted to get annoyed, but don't become dejected, as he is. Lay down your cards petulantly, not soulfully, in something after this fashion: "Well, there seems to be no pleasing you today! I have been pleasant as I could, but you are apparently determined to be dull, so I shall go and spend my time in more responsive company. Let us meet again when you feel more amiable!" And with that, you take steps for your immediate departure.

The accusation of dullness from one who is usually flattering will put him on his mettle. Even if, an instant before, he had felt no desire ever to see you again, his vanity will not let you go away under the impression that he is dull. He will want to prove the reverse at once, or at least offer you some explanation as to why he is so. The explanation will probably not be the true one, but in trying to convince you that he has a headache, or an attack of nerves, or something of the kind, he will convince himself. Or suppose he is not roused immediately to detain you and explain himself, your remark about meeting again when he feels more amiable will almost certainly be acted upon—that is, unless he has positively turned against you, which is not likely without an adequate reason.

Perhaps you would care to hear how an incompetent woman would behave on finding her admirer in such a mood as I have described. To begin with, she would persist in asking him a dozen times what was the matter with him—had she offended him?[5] Was he upset about something? As he repeatedly assured her that there was nothing the matter, he would grow more and more antipathetic, until, out of sheer exasperation, he might at last blurt out whatever slight irritation or embarrassment was on his mind, and the very act of putting it into words would lend it weight and impetus. She would rightly feel that she was losing him, and in her fear of letting him be the first to sever

■

[5] *To begin with, she would persist . . .*

Almost every couple can recognize themselves in this classic scenario: The woman pleads, "What's wrong?" The man, clearly aggrieved, replies, "Nothing." Women tend to belong to the "talking it over" school of problem solving, while men withdraw from emotional "scenes." The silent male retains the power, while his partner grows increasingly frantic. But the woman who can gracefully withdraw will disarm her opponent and enhance her prestige.

Q. *May I call upon a young woman whom I greatly admire, although she had not given me the permission? Would she be flattered at my eagerness, even to the setting aside of conventions, or would she think me impertinent?*

A. *I think that you would risk her just displeasure and frustrate your object of finding favor with her. An invitation might be secured through a mutual friend.*

—Ladies' Home Journal, 1909

■

[6]*Lastly, there is the mismanagement of a parting . . .*

With the advent of modern dating, control passed to masculine hands. In *From Front Porch to Back Seat* (1988), Beth Bailey writes: "Dating moved courtship out of the home and into man's sphere—the world outside the home." Single women found themselves in alien territory where men set the rules. Transgressors were labeled "forward," "desperate" or, most damning of all, "fast." Those unable to convey interest through guile were forced into helpless silence.

Under the new paradigm, partings left women especially vulnerable. Dorothy Parker describes the independent woman torn between her loneliness and the social imperative to appear cheery, carefree, and desired:

"When will I see you again?" she said.

"I'll call you up," he said. "I'm all tied up at the office and everything. Tell you what I'll do. I'll give you a ring."

"Honestly, I have more dates!" she said. "It's terrible. I don't know when I'll have a minute. But you call up, will you?"

"I'll do that," he said. . . .

the thread between them, she would do so herself by casting an air of finality upon the meeting, of which he, half unconsciously, would take advantage.

If you want to keep up a light affair—one in which you are bound rather by silken threads than by the strong cords of many joys and griefs shared—never, never let a bad humour lead you into parting with the manner of one saying a last farewell. Never indicate the end unnecessarily. A flirtation should be a kind of serial story; each instalment should break off at a promising juncture, leaving a man wondering whether the next will finish his suspense or merely increase it.

In this chapter I have warned you against seven dangers. I shall set them down again in a few words, because, trivial as they sound, they are of immense significance. First, it is dangerous to model yourself upon what a man tells you of his tastes, especially if he profess only virtuous preferences. Secondly, you expose yourself to risk when you grant important favours in any other hour than the exactly propitious one, which generally is brought about by careful preparation. The third and fourth dangers are somewhat similar: these are, the danger of not letting emotion rest when it is tired, and the danger of demanding perpetual verbal confirmation of a lover's devotion.

The fifth is the undue self-consciousness which causes you to draw attention to your defects, and the sixth is the foolishness of confiding matters about yourself which, though not in the nature of faults, are still more liable to jeopardise your prestige.

Lastly, there is the mismanagement of a parting,[6] either

by openly requesting another meeting, or openly revealing the fact that you do not expect one.

You will marvel, perhaps, that I have left out some errors which I have heavily stressed elsewhere, such as the habit of letting a man know that his companionship is of greater moment to you than yours to him, or indelicacy, or masculinity, or excessive emotion. These matters cannot be classed as dangerous, however. They are simply fatal, and that is why I have omitted them.

Even today, a woman who openly asks a man for a date defies convention. In an informal roundtable discussion reported in *Elle* magazine in 1996, single men admitted they found it flattering to be asked out. But as soon as the moderator broached the subject, they nervously began talking about obsessive, pushy women—the underlying assumption being that an assertive woman is unnatural and threatening. In her very directness, she usurps men's traditional role as pursuer, making them feel vulnerable. Men may complain of having to do all the "work" and risk rejection, but the "work" gives them control.

Cosmetics

"Why do you put that stuff on your face?" . . . (p. 155)
It seems that women have always "painted" to attract
men and that men have always complained about it, even
while they were attracted to it. They charged that a
painted woman was unnatural, and hence deceptive.
Shakespeare compared a made-up woman to a hybrid
flower created by gardeners instead of by God. In his
mock love poem, "A Beautiful Young Nymph Going to
Bed," Swift exposed and denounced female artifice. He
portrayed an aging prostitute preparing for bed, remov-
ing her false body parts, wiping her features clean, and
finally revealing the balding crone beneath the feathers
and false hair.

Victorian women painted discreetly; they reddened
their lips and cheeks with carmine and dropped bel-
ladonna in their eyes to dilate their pupils and make them
glisten. The overall effect was supposed to simulate
nature (and, more particularly, says Diane Ackerman,
the state of sexual arousal)—sparkling eyes and bloom-

ing cheeks and lips—"as God intended" but did not, alas, endow. The less daring achieved a similar effect by pinching their cheeks and biting their lips; others indulged in an inexplicable process called enameling. Until the turn of the century, obvious makeup (like dyed hair) advertised a woman's sexual availability. By the 1920s cosmetics had shed their moral implications—the lady of fashion was a creature of design. A compact was now an *objet* to be displayed, not hidden. The female face was a blank canvas to be lacquered and adorned. Eyes, encircled with black, were raccoonlike; brows, plucked thin, arched high over the bone; lips were shaped into a pouty Cupid's bow and reddened. The finished product was a provocative, inscrutable mask. In *Seeing Through Clothes* (1975), Anne Hollander writes:

> The results were often in fact quite extreme and abstract, and they never fooled anyone; but writers who attacked cosmetics loved to point this out as if it were a failure of the original purpose. After 1920, however, modern makeup confessed itself to be the kind of paint modern artists were using, not for creating artificial reality but for design.

Eleven

...

A little sincerity is a dangerous thing, and a great
deal of it is absolutely fatal.

—OSCAR WILDE, *The Critic as Artist*, 1891

CYPRIA   As you are never likely to experience a love affair wholly free from disagreements, you will do well to furnish yourself in advance with the effective manner of offering a rebuke or remonstrance. An occasional dissension is an almost necessary variation in the even ebb and flow of courtship, if only for the delight of "making it up."

Now, tears should not be used as reproaches save in the direst extremity, or when they are quite patently produced at will. You may cry in a childish, pouting way because you are refused a new dress, for instance, and the obvious femininity of that wile will serve you well—if you don't overwork it. But never weep grievously before a man while there is any other way of obtaining what you want from him. Though heaving sobs and swollen eyes will almost invariably gain the day for you,[1] the victory will cost you so much prestige that only the most vital cause could be worth it. However, if a time should arrive when you cannot prevent tears from falling, I invoke you to make your misery as picturesque as possible.

You will understand that the tears I warn you to suppress are those directed at a man in some kind of reproof or appeal, not those that spring from sympathy for him or for

■

[1] *Though heaving sobs and swollen eyes . . .*

The tearful, clinging woman in Dorothy Parker's "A Telephone Call" stories is a case study in "How Not to Do It."

They don't like you to tell them they've made you cry. They don't like you to tell them you're unhappy because of them. If you do, they think you're possessive and exacting. And then they hate you.

They hate you whenever you say anything you really think. You always have to keep playing little games.

According to Deborah Tannen, some men view the "knock-down, drag-out" fights as a form of "ritual combat and value it as a form of involvement," while women avoid conflict, preferring instead those long talks that men dread.

any other creature. I would not have you cold and insensible. It is advisable, I think, to be entirely gay during the period of approach, but when that shallow time is over, there is no necessity to conceal the effect wrought upon your tenderness by what is pathetic—so long, of course, as you are not incessantly lachrymose.

Open contempt and ridicule are common forms of rebuke, but always odious, especially when administered in the presence of others. I have heard many a woman boasting of how she made a man "feel small"—not a man whom she wished to be rid of, I assure you, but one whom she expressly intended to retain. If there be anything on earth repugnant to a masculine creature, it is a woman who addresses him with asperity, sarcasm, or laughing derision before her friends or his. Even good-humoured mockery should not be too frequently employed against men. It may have a good and salutary effect upon *them*, but it will make *you* peculiarly unpopular.

If your admirer does or says something which is distasteful to you, you may reprove him with as much heat or coldness as you please—since you, Saccharissa, will be able to grow angry without becoming inelegant—but confine yourself to the actual annoyance in question, utter no belittling comments upon his conduct in general, nor embarrassing reminders of events past and gone, and above all, express your temper in private. But these remarks should be almost unnecessary, since they constitute the true etiquette of quarrelling between all well-mannered persons, lovers or otherwise.

And even in a state of antagonism you need not cease to be flattering, for you can intersperse your complaints with: "I never would have expected it of you!" "*You* whom I have always looked up to!" and many other softening amenities. Thus, when the quarrel is over, neither will carry away from it anything that will rankle in the memory.

You may sometimes have to deal with offences that are not isolated errors of judgment or taste, but an irritating habit which you notice with more and more exasperation. A man may be conspicuously rude to his social inferiors, or indelicate in his talk, or excessive in his drinking, or careless of his appearance; in fact, there are a thousand displeasing traits or mannerisms, of which he can have quite a number and yet remain attractive enough to inspire in you a longing for his improvement. Well, there is a method of correction upon the efficacy of which I will stake my repute as a technician, but to bring it into play you must not shrink from arch-hypocrisy. This method simply consists of telling him at every opening that he has *not* got the very fault which is racking your nerves.

To illustrate, let us suppose that you wish to marry a man who has an inclination to be miserly, an objectionable quality in anyone, and unspeakable in a future husband. Instead of confirming him in his vice by any sign of having observed it, either with resentment or approbation, you should take pains to instil into him very gradually the idea that he is an unusually generous fellow. You might begin with a few remarks, uttered entirely without special emphasis, in this spirit: "If there is one vice I detest, it is meanness! Thank

Heaven that is not one of your faults, because if it were, I could not have become fond of you, I'm sure."

Assuming that he has not yet reached a stage where he glories in avarice, he will naturally not attempt to contradict your good opinion, and it will doubtless have the effect of making him a little more open-handed, at least towards you. By degrees, and with great tact, you can praise him definitely for his liberality, expressing a conviction that he will always be as lavish in his hospitality as his means will permit, and will treat everybody handsomely—especially his wife. You may be certain that, in the course of time, he will learn to live up to his reputation, and you, as his reformer, will be entitled to the just reward of your perseverance.

As for a man whose bad tendency is already fully developed, light artifices would, of course, be unavailing. I have already given you a warning against entering into any intimacy with one who is hardened in vice, but it might unluckily happen that, before you discover his unfitness for you, you have already become entangled with him; and in this event, albeit the likelihood of reclaiming him is not great, you will probably wish to make an effort. Then your most difficult task will be to restrain yourself from harping incessantly upon the theme of his delinquencies. You might succeed by this practice in making him vividly aware of his degradation, but you could never cure him of it. You would only cause him to become depressed, and, perhaps, to turn to his favourite excesses in order to forget himself. The best reformers are those who emphasise the joys of virtue than the squalors of vice.

For misconducts which have an absolutely direct bearing upon the trend of your love affair, as distinct from the oblique matters of which we have spoken, the best kind of admonition is generally that which takes the same shape as the offence. When a man pays undue attentions to other women, you must appear interested in other men; if he neglects you, he in his turn must be neglected; if he excludes you from his pleasures, exclude him utterly from yours. This method, if he is genuinely attached to you at heart, will not fail of effect, and if he is indifferent and perhaps waiting for an excuse for parting from you, yours is the satisfaction of having prevented the affair from lingering on in a moribund condition.

I will dare to boast that if you were to conduct your amatory affairs from their very inception upon these principles, you would never have cause to fear the loss of a suitor, or need to know any tactics for a time when his devotion recedes to an alarmingly low ebb. It is possible, however, that you may err through want of faith in my counsels or imperfect apprehension of them, and therefore it will not be out of place to consider the question of dealing with a lover who has clearly grown apathetic. Whatever hurt it may inflict on you, there is then but one course which will save you the mortification of being deserted, and that is deserting him first.

Never remonstrate with a man whose desire is flagging. Cease to see him, cease to communicate with him, and if it is feasible, let a rumour or two be conveyed to him—false, if you cannot make it true—that you are seen with others,

■

²*. . . recollect that you must not . . .*

Few writers have illustrated the dangers of emotional indiscretion better than Jane Austen—particularly in *Sense and Sensibility*. Marianne Dashwood's behavior at a London party should send a *frisson* of embarrassed recognition down the spine of anyone who has ever bared her heart to an indifferent lover. Spying her lover at a London party, she demands an explanation for his neglect. "Good God, Willoughby, what is the meaning of this?" His cool brush-off and her repeated entreaties only make matters worse: Unable to adopt the pose of lighthearted composure, Marianne "gives way to the misery of her feelings. . . ." while exposing herself to the pity and amusement of the other guests.

■

³*But what if you should be the first to tire? . . .*

A flapper's rebuff to an unwanted advance:

    Applesauce!
    So's your anchovie!
    Banana oil!
    Chew to the line!
    Let the hips fall where they
will!

care-free and pleasure-seeking. Be sure that if he has any lingering residue of possessive passion for you, these measures will bring him back to your side, and if he has not, you are acquitted without indignity.

Above all, recollect that you must not,[2] by complaints of his coldness and tearful requests for explanations, precipitate a scene in which he will be forced uncomfortably to declare his change of feeling, for then he will always remember your parting with embarrassment, and nothing could be more injurious to your confidence in yourself than to know there is a man in existence who would cross a street to avoid meeting you. Let your relations with men leave memories of seething fury and hatred rather than embarrassment.

Should your lover be stimulated by the relics of jealousy to return to you, let his reception be somewhat cool. Be very slow to take him back into your good graces after he has once shown himself faithless or neglectful. No man shall be able to say or think that he discarded you, if you adopt these old but never obsolete devices.

But what if you should be the first to tire?[3] Or if a still fervent admirer should become a liability rather than an asset? I need hardly ask you to "let him down" as lightly as you can. Your state of mind should not be put into words, except when he happens to be an extremely objectionable or persistent man: the gentlest speech within the range of eloquence must wound deeply when, in effect, it says, "I have grown so tired of you that all your advances bore me," or "Your manner of making love offends my susceptibilities, and your admiration does not contribute to my prestige, so I wish to be rid of you."

Rather tell the lie which, though it will give pain, can cause no such desperate humiliation as the truth: say that you have fallen in love with someone else. I know of no surer and kinder way of ending an attachment than this. You do not have to justify yourself by showing him his own shortcomings, and thus all can be made to end in amity. True, a man's pride (the chief source of torment in love affairs) will suffer when he thinks you have found more attraction in another, but how much worse are its pangs when he is told that his own lack of attraction, not someone else's excess of it, has resulted in his defeat! It is to be remarked too that no man remains long in love with a woman whose sexual allurements are all, as he imagines, directed at another person.

I have often been obliged to repress a smile when some woman has said to me, "Do you know, I simply can't get rid of that man. I give him absolutely no encouragement—I have tried my very best to refuse his invitations and so forth, but still he is always hanging on to me." Real aloofness—that which is just unmistakably cold, not that which is tantalising—is in itself quite sufficient to dampen any ardour in the course of time, and a woman who protests in the style I have quoted has certainly attempted to keep her pursuer at arms' length after a fashion well calculated to heighten the effect of her charms.

I have noticed in our sex a kind of feebleness—or would you say reluctance to give pain, Saccharissa?—which produces a tendency to compromise. We find it intolerably difficult to take earnest steps towards breaking off a relation. We will go on for years passively enduring the company of a man we have grown to detest rather than gather together strength of mind enough to sever the attachment once and for all. I have observed as well a lamentable habit in us of behaving like the ill-famed dog in the manger. Little as we may want a certain admirer ourselves, we cannot bear any-one else to get him. I have known women who for years have put themselves to the greatest inconvenience to pre-vent others from attaining men for whom they felt not a single amorous pulsation.

Of course, you cannot be expected to set an admirer free merely because you are not actually in love with him, or to please some jealous creature whom you like better. There should be at least two men desiring you at one time—more if you are very skilful or fortunate. To have three or four willing to dance attendance on you is indeed to be invincible.

Now, you might argue: "I cannot have more than one love affair at a time without being unfaithful to each of the men who are concerned in them, and yet to tell me that I should punish a man who is unfaithful to me! Can this be fair?" It is better than fair, it is poetic justice; for is it not right that we should compensate ourselves for being physi-cally in bondage while men are free, by allowing *our* pas-sions to roam at liberty while we hold theirs enslaved?

Nevertheless, it is only the flirtation that I advise you to multiply, not a relation with the magnitude of a love affair. It is a foolish practice to have more than one of these in progress at the same time, unless, being adept at intrigue, you can consistently screen each from the other; and that can scarcely be managed without lying, and deception, which is a very bad policy if you wish for lasting successes. Discretion is to be cultivated, but deceit is seriously demoralising. Yet if you conducted, say, two affairs with openness, neither could be of long duration. No normal man who is in love will tolerate such a situation for more than a short time. Beyond a certain point, jealousy stifles rather than quickens the breath of passion.

Your love affair should be hedged about with flirtations, and your lover should believe—preferably with accuracy—that several others would clamour for his place of favour and intimacy if he relaxed his hold upon you. But, though you should find means to display your admirer to your lover, you must not flaunt your lover before your admirers. (Interpret "lover" in any way you choose, so long as it implies the most favoured of those who surround you.) You see, a man who seeks after you will not mind having to compete with others who are no further advanced in your regard than himself, but when he observes that most of your attention is already focussed upon someone else, and imagines how small his share will be, vanity alone will check his pursuit. Therefore, if lover and admirers meet together, do not show that you incline more responsively to the one than to the others.

If it is a husband who happens to be present among those who stand for lighter diversion, you need not—if he be well trained—use any tactics at all, except to show him up at his best, so that he does you credit.[4] A husband who excites the contempt of your companions will sadly detract from your prestige, and you will have to keep him out of

■

[4]*If it is a husband who happens to be present* . . .

Cypria's affected casualness, a self-conscious blend of Oscar Wilde, Bernard Shaw, and Noël Coward, reflects the temper of her time and class. The well-educated aristocrats, known as the "Bright Young People," adopted a determinedly frivolous attitude toward the sanctities of wedlock. A husband may be a necessity, but he should always be made to feel expendable.

LADY CAROLINE: *What stuff and nonsense all this about men is! The thing to do is to keep men in their proper place.*
MRS. ALLONBY: *But what is their proper place, Lady Caroline?*
LADY CAROLINE: *Looking after their wives.*

—Oscar Wilde,
A Woman of No Importance, 1893

sight, which is a pity. Should he be creditable to your taste and powers, however, and be not opposed to your pleasantly enjoying yourself, you may bring him among your admirers without hesitation. He will not frighten them away as an openly acknowledged lover would. Only the very timorous now are frightened by a husband.

Twelve

■ ■ ■

And I'm going to tell you a secret now.
It's about girls and how they dress and how they
do their hair. Men always think these things are
frivolous matters. Nothing could be further from
the truth. The girl in the red dress with the
plunging neckline may be only shopping for a
washing machine as she tangos so sensually upon
the dance floor. She may know very well that it
takes this dress to get that fellow to let her wash
those clothes in that washing machine he's going
to buy her when they are married.

—VINA DELMAR,
"Midnight of a Bridesmaid,"
in *Ladies' Home Journal,* March 1955,
cited by Beth Bailey in *From Front Porch
to Backseat,* 1988

CYPRIA After a time you may wish for a flirtation to become a love affair, or for a love affair to lead to marriage [see On the Proposal *at the end of this chapter*]. To achieve the first purpose you have merely to become bolder and more physical in your allurements, less superficial and more intimate, and nothing could be easier. For unless you have misjudged the situation entirely, your admirer, once he is given the opportunity, will assist you at every turn. The second purpose requires deeper craftsmanship, and it must be my final task to instruct you in it.

Your best plan is to awaken in the man's breast a sense of responsibility—a pleasant, not an irksome, feeling that he has duties towards you. I need hardly say that never as long as you live should you make yourself a nuisance under any provocation, but if you wish to take a vital part in his life, you cannot always remain (what you must seem at first) a light diversion which he can enjoy while he is free as air. Stealthily you must work your way into those schemes of his which are real and earnest.

It may happen that a man, though sufficiently attracted to you to seek out your company and protest his affection, yet shows no all-conquering craving to be wedded to you. He will probably be self-conscious on the topic, and offer, truthfully or otherwise, some reason why marriage is not in his power, alleging social or financial disparity, parental opposition, or the like. But do not be disarmed by specious excuses, though he believe them himself. Smug and solemn as it may seem, it is a part of my undertaking to assure you that if a man loves you, or—under the influence of physical attraction—imagines he loves you, and if marriage is remotely within his power, he will endeavour to marry you. Now, as at any other period of Western history, you must place no reliance on the ardour of a man who does not express this wish.

It may be true that Nature intended us to be polygamous, and that no one can safely promise fidelity for the rest of his days; but when we are in love, we *believe* that we shall never want anyone else again, and we have no hesitation in pledging ourselves to this faith. Not everybody who marries is in love, but everybody who is in love is willing to marry if circumstances allow. Even those who would reform or abolish matrimony,[1] and who hold it responsible for the many evils and hypocrisies of our social system—even they are prone to forsake their principles when they are seized with a passion for one who cannot be otherwise obtained.

You will observe that word "otherwise." The fact that a woman will not be possessed save in marriage often causes desire to take on such magnitude that a man becomes willing to pay that unlimited price for his gratification; and conversely, the same degree of desire, if granted in a manner which is called illicit, will be at least partially quenched.

■

[1] *Even those who would . . .*

The scholar Denis de Rougement maintains that the persistent hope that marriage will secure passion lies at the source of marital woe. We marry to safeguard the transient emotion that marriage inevitably destroys. Perhaps there would be less divorce if couples approached wedlock with less ardor and more irony.

And where it vanishes, cold reason appears. Let us admit, however reluctantly, that cold reason can seldom recommend marriage, with all its fetters, to free, untrammelled man, and that we have usually to take him either by storm or by enchantment. Your surest weapon and your most powerful spell lie in his own hunger for possession of you, and so the obvious conclusion is one which will gratify even the most fastidious: that is, excellent Saccharissa, that until you have fulfilled your ambition, you should always be unattainable—at any rate, to the men whom you find particularly eligible.

But desire in its physical sense is not all that I mean when I speak of the great incentive to matrimony. It should not stand alone, and very rarely does. There is also a longing for intimacy of mind and life, and for the authorised right to "cherish and protect." Your suitor should, in short, have a sentiment as well as a passion for you, and it is this which results in the sense of responsibility I have mentioned. There are little ways of inspiring that feeling.

If you exact a certain amount of cherishing and protection in small things, and receive it enjoyably, he will come to consider that it would be delightful to be held accountable for you in all things. If you draw him into slight intimacies that seem charming, his mind will turn to deep intimacies that promise to be more charming still. If you subtly reveal to him little bonds between you which are pleasant, he will be eager to be bound more closely, and with stronger ties.

Acquiring a husband who does not approach to Hymen[2]

■

[2]*Hymen* . . .
   In Greek mythology, the god of marriage, who appears at the wedding feast to bless the union.

spontaneously is often what may be termed a "confidence trick." (Remember my obligation to speak plainly, and forgive the crudity, I beg!) You have to convince him against his judgment that he is devoted to you, and unable to do without you. It is as though you were to keep on saying: "Come, you know I am indispensable to you. You had better make sure of me by marriage, for that's the only way." If by your attitude you reiterate this often enough, and attractively too, you will be believed.

Jealousy can be made to serve you in the delicate art of suggestion. In an earlier passage I remarked upon jealousy on your part as a sign of over-anxiety, and therefore destructive to prestige. There is one stage in the love affair, however, when to display a discreet kind of jealousy actually adds to your prestige, or when not to do so would be to injure it. You see, in the beginning you are to conceal whatever chagrin his partiality for others causes you, because you must not give away too early your own partiality for him. But later, after you have both declared yourselves, he would hold you cheaply indeed if you showed yourself willing to share his favours with others.

You may have your little fits of jealousy then, and they will help to remind him of what ties there are between you; but take care that they are of the wilful, petulant or teasing variety, and not charged with sincere and hence dangerous emotion. I might almost say, you must veil any real jealousies and exhibit only such as are fictitious and can therefore be treated quite artificially and prettily. Pretend to resent attachments which are non-existent, or which you know you could overthrow in a moment, but lie low when you are doubtful of your supremacy. Do not court comparisons unless you are very sure of holding your own.

You are well aware by now that you should never put into a man's head an idea which may prove disadvantageous to you, an idea, for example, that he finds a certain other woman more fascinating than yourself, that he will be unfaithful to you at the first provocation, and so forth. I have told you that most men will give you whatever you seem to expect of them. If you seriously show that you expect infidelity, that is what you will most decidedly be given. Be on guard against emphasising the charms of a potential rival by exposing a fear of them. The safest course is silence. You must not call attention to her either by praise or by contumely.

Now as to arousing jealousy in your suitor, all my counsel, I think, has tended to show that in a greater or less degree this must be an almost perpetual condition. (In the stronghold of wifehood, you can afford to relax from time to time, I agree, but with all your threads in your hand, ready to be manipulated at an instant's notice.)

I don't mean that by repeated acts of inconstancy you should for ever be causing pain. Such tactics, while they might stimulate him to infatuation at first, would ultimately goad him to defiance and vengefulness, and he would assuredly live to hoist you with your own petard.

You ought not to inflict jealousy of a sharp and bitter sort upon him save as the punishment of neglect or self-conceit. For ordinary purposes, he should consider, not that you *are*

■

³*For ordinary purposes* . . .

Proust maintained that a subtle threat of infidelity hovers over every successful marriage. The most indifferent husband can be roused when confronted by loss—imagined or real. He may no longer love his wife, but until he gets her back, he'll feel as if he does. As the genius of lost time, Proust was also the great anatomist of possessive jealousy, a feeling evoked by the fear of loss. In each volume of *Remembrance of Things Past*, Marcel, Proust's fictional alter-ego, examines the lover's psyche, his tormented yearning to possess the beloved who, he suspects, is poised on the verge of flight. Thus in *The Captive*, Marcel recalls: "[Albertine] had promised us a letter, we were calm. No messenger appears with it; what can have happened? Anxiety is born afresh, and love." The yearning for the inaccessible, whether for a lover or the irretrievable past, inspires love and great art.

unfaithful to him, but that you *might* be if he ceased for an hour to deserve your good graces.³ He should be dimly conscious of a sense of insecurity, and he should fear the machinations of other men. Only thus can you keep him flatteringly vigilant.

Whenever you have reason to believe that he is swayed by some influence adverse to you, make haste to have the first word in using the self-same influence against him. Remember the excellent, if ancient, stratagem of always taking the offensive when you fear to be assailed.

This is a policy that will aid you signally if ever you should harbour conjugal intentions towards someone who may feel debarred from marriage by external interference. Parental opposition on his side, for example, is a very likely contingency, since mothers rarely let their sons marry without a struggle; and if mismanaged, it might well militate against your prospects. But a clever woman will always enlist it as her ally, and turn to great advantage every attempt to come between her lover and herself.

Do not give him the opportunity of telling you that he is not in a position to ask you to be his wife: instead, when you fancy that he is about to do so, inform him that you would never become the wife of a man in his position. I certainly do not mean that you should make it possible for him to retort, with nursery rhyme impoliteness: "Nobody asked you!" I am assuming, firstly, that you know definitely that he cares for you more than for any other woman, even though he is not yet at that high-strung pitch of desire where he will fight against any obstacles in order to possess you; and secondly, that you have enough invention to find some excuse for interpolating such a statement into your conversation, and in an artless, matter-of-fact manner.

Supposing then that you are acquainted with his parents, or at any rate with their views, and can rely on their being hostile to the alliance you contemplate, "Now, *you* are the last person I could marry," you might say quite casually when you happen to be discussing that commonest of topics. "I should never, never accept a man in the face of objections from his family, and I am sure that yours would object."

If he has ever had the slightest notion that it would be pleasant to marry you, the assurance that his chances are already foredoomed through your knowledge of his parents will cause him to be annoyed with them. Very, very gradually, your variations on this theme will make him feel that his family is thwarting him, and that it is almost incumbent upon him to defy them.

In the case of a man who proposes marriage to you first, and discovers afterwards the hostility of his family, which you perceive to be affecting him unfavourably, do not—like so many excellent but pitifully misguided women—do not, I beg, say staunchly: "Never mind, dear, we'll get on in spite of them as best we can. I'll stand by you whatever happens." If it is inconvenient to oppose his family, he may eventually decide that in standing by him you are really a millstone round his neck. Your proper policy will be to reply, after a little significant hesitation, in a tremulous but noble speech, something after this style: "Well, I'm afraid there is nothing to do but to part. I should never wish to stand in your light with your people, or to come among them as an intruder. If they are determined to choose your

wife for you, you must let them have their way. Nothing would induce me to marry you against their will, so let us say good-bye and forget about each other."

What man worthy the name will accept his dismissal thus when he believes you still care for him? What man, even if he had been almost resigned to giving you up before, but will be spurred on to break down the domestic opposition by a super-human effort, or, should that prove useless, to marry you in spite of opposition? And do you think that when you had changed your mind, and took him after all without the family blessing, he would hold you less dear for it? Not at all. Caprice, you must remember, is your prerogative.

I will not treat of opposition from your family, for with our sex so horridly in the majority, a girl's parents or guardians do not usually put forward many obstacles to her match with a tolerably eligible man. And unless it is such a one as this that you decide to espouse in the absolute certainty of success, I shall consider my pains all wasted.

On the Proposal

After a time you may wish . . . (p. 185)
In fiction (and sometimes in life) a marriage proposal is the triumphant realization of a woman's aspirations and schemes. Victorian proposals followed strict protocol: The suitor first met with his prospective father-in-law to declare his intentions and disclose his financial condition. Only with permission could he then propose to the young lady in question—who was usually waiting in the next room. When she consented, reticence briefly gave way and a chaste kiss sealed the match.

In *The Importance of Being Earnest,* Oscar Wilde subverts Victorian formalities: His heroine prompts her lover, and before he can utter a word, accepts him. This anti-love scene concludes with her remark, "I am afraid you have had very little experience in how to propose."

By 1918, proposals had become less momentous, and the roles assigned to the sexes less clearly defined. In his short story "Love in the Slump," Evelyn Waugh describes Angela, an aging debutante of twenty-five:

"Faced with the grim prospect of prolonged residence in the home of her ancestors," she accosts an old chum and pops the question herself. The heroine of D. H. Lawrence's *Women in Love* is indignant when her lover (with whom she is intimate) pays a formal visit to her father: "Why should I say anything," she cries. "Why do you both want to bully me?" The novels of Jane Austen, Dickens, and the Brontës conclude with the proposal and marriage of the hero and heroine, and we rarely consider what happens to them next. Marriage provides closure in narrative, but not in life. In the more realistic modern novels such as those by Lawrence or Forster, the proposal is merely part of the story, not its conclusion.

Thirteen

. . .

A woman can look both moral and exciting—if
she also looks as if it was quite a struggle.

—EDNA FERBER,
Reader's Digest, December 1954

CYPRIA When you have finally decided to be married, it is essential, I think, to enlighten your prospective husband upon any incidents in your past which he might resent if he heard them from other lips than your own. I need not put this to you, my honourable friend, in its ethical aspect; I mention it simply as a matter of technique. You see, an incident of this nature which had been concealed would look far more serious when found out than it need have done; and moreover, to make a confession is to make a bond. I really pity you if you have nothing of any gravity to confess:[1] a man in love will be so delighted by your daring confidence, and by the high-minded scruple which prompts you to pour it into his ear, that his devotion will increase in the most charming manner.

There should be no Lady Dedlocks nowadays,[2] guarding in desperate ways the dark, unutterable secret of having had a lover before marriage. And guarding it, I doubt not in most cases, from husbands who had practised in their youth all the dissipations then in fashion. The cultured men of this generation are almost wholly converted to the justice of not demanding more purity from a wife than they bring to her. If she has lived in spotless virtue, well and good; if she has not, let her only choose the perfect moment for her expla-

■

[1] *I really pity you . . .*
Confession marked a crucial and final stage of the courtship process and could make or break a future marriage, depending on the man's capacity for mercy. This dramatic moment was a pivotal point in hundreds of marriage plots in fiction and plays and the subject of numerous paintings. These Victorian Magdalens appear anguished, their moist eyes pleading for forgiveness.

The modern confession, as advocated by Cypria, is part of a flapper's technique—a nod to convention and male prudery. It could also enhance a woman's appeal by making her seem both virtuous *and* experienced.

■

[2] *. . . Lady Dedlocks . . .*
Honoria Dedlock, mother of the novel's illegitimate heroine in Charles Dickens's *Bleak House*. When threatened with public disgrace, she flees from her home and dies from exposure.

nation, and all will be understood. A marked craving to mate with chastity is a common feature of sensual and debauched men, and that is no doubt why our forefathers, who drank so hard, and seduced so many servant girls, were very particular as to the spotlessness of the women they wedded.

I do not for a moment belittle the value of chastity. It is so simple, so clearly the line of least resistance. Life is immeasurably more hazardous and complex for an unmarried woman who has flung down the barrier of maidenhood. But though by doing so she discards a powerful protection, her experience, if she is discriminating, will increase her skill and furnish her with new blandishments. An analogy might be drawn from the warriors of ancient times who, totally encased in armour, were certainly well guarded from receiving an injury, yet without it might have been far more agile, subtle, and dexterous.

It was through the wiles of chaste women,[3] I imagine, that a man first learned to consider his honour sullied by union with one who had already known some sexual adventure: they were aware—those guileful virgins—that they could not compete with sophistication while they wore their cumbersome armour, and, since armour was too safe to be abandoned, there was nothing to do but to make sophistication disgraceful.

Of course, the strange notions of "fallen women," "guilty love," and "lives of sin," which were so universal only a few decades ago, cannot be utterly erased from the mind in one or two generations. Young men smile healthily at their grandsires' codes, but in the undercurrents of

[3]*It was through the wiles of chaste women . . .*

Cypria's detached attitude toward virginity is part of the tendency of the day to challenge taboos and customs that once seemed self-evident and inviolable. According to anthropologists and psychoanalysts, virginity arose out of social, commercial, and psychological considerations rather than any ingrained ethical imperative.

The demand for sexual purity is a vestige of a time when marriage was an economic transaction and a husband literally owned his wife, much as he did any other "chattel." Occasionally one still hears a sexually experienced woman referred to as a commodity—as "shopworn" or "damaged goods."

Woman's virtue is man's greatest invention.
—Cornelia Otis Skinner, *Paris '90,* 1952

THE TECHNIQUE OF THE LOVE AFFAIR

thought faint traces of them remain, and to these we must make certain concessions. We must pretend that we were the seduced, not (as is so often the case) the seducers, and we must say that we are sorry, and that it shall not occur again. The time is not ripe yet, I think, to talk boldly, face to face, of our right to sexual experience. We may do so impersonally through the medium of literature and art, but even today it might be regarded as a little destructive to feminine charm to announce an individual claim to such a right; and it is the charm, not the emancipation of our sex, which is the subject of this work.

It is not advisable, as I hinted in the last chapter, to take more than a small part of that experience with the man whom you wish to marry, until your mating has been duly sanctioned and solemnised—not because he will necessarily respect you less afterwards, but simply because he will desire you less, and will therefore feel less inducement to bind himself to you for a period extending—nominally, at least—till death. Even if in the test of possession he finds that you satisfy his most extravagant ideals, still his curiosity for physical knowledge of you will be appeased, and that forms no inconsiderable portion of desire.

It is by no means to be inferred from this that a man never marries a woman if he can obtain her without doing so. I am well aware that numerous unions are rooted in genuine affection between people who really find each other intensely congenial, and who want to live together for the sake of unrestricted companionship. I am also prepared to admit half-a-dozen other excellent reasons for getting married. There is the leaning towards comfortable domesticity

Was such hypocrisy still necessary? In this anomic age, a man might profess an enlightened attitude about female sexuality, while clinging to traditional ideals of female purity. If a suitor is sympathetic, confession erases the past, giving the supplicant a second chance, and indeed, essentially restoring her lost virginity.

You could become a virgin again. She finally understood that it was a man's word. They didn't mean you had done it once; they meant you did it, the lost hymen testimony not of the past but the present. . . .
—Andre Dubus,
"Graduation," 1988

completed by children—not a very common motive in young men. There is the terror of loneliness in old age, but that likewise does not affect the young. There is the need for a wife to help in supporting one's social position, or for an heir to inherit one's wealth or rank—but how many have these requirements before middle age? A few who are weak-willed or exceptionally good-natured will marry because they see it is expected of them, a few because they hope to find in matrimony a salvation from some vice which preys upon them, and some because it is for them a good business arrangement.

But who will deny that possessive desire must be held responsible for by far the greatest proportion of marriages? Therefore any attitude which nourishes but does not satisfy it is to be recommended, and any other is to be avoided.

If the tone of your confidence be correct and your suitor a gentleman, have no fear of his unreasonably insisting that since you have yielded to another, or others, you can yield to him.

Select for your avowal the most opportune moment that can arise. Let it be one of undisturbed tranquillity, when you are entirely sure of his affection, and preferably soon after you have promised to marry him. Tell him that you have something on your conscience which alters everything. I will even allow you, on this special occasion, to shed a few tears. Make your confession, throw yourself upon his tenderness. Absolution will not be withheld from you. An Angel Clare today would be a curious anachronism.[4]

If a man discards a woman for an offence which in these

[4] *Angel Clare* . . .
Tess Durbeyfield's husband, the embodiment of the double standard, in Thomas Hardy's *Tess of the D'Urbervilles*. Tess's famous confession takes place on her wedding night. Heartened by Angel's avowal of his sins, Tess tells her own sorry tale. When she pleads for mercy, he replies, "O Tess, forgiveness does not apply in the case! You were one person, now you are another."

Can a woman today still have what was once darkly referred to as a "Past"? Apparently so. The agonizing question, To tell or not to tell, still pops up in advice columns and radio talk shows. But more often than not, "Scared in Sacramento" is advised to keep her own counsel on the rationale that a woman's history is no one's business but her own.

days is nothing weighed against a real attachment, he has been secretly waiting for an excuse to break away from her. He may disguise the fact to himself, and believe in the motive he professes, but a sincere affection, or a vivid desire for possession, will not succumb to a single blow. Both can be slowly strangled by a great number of petty irritations; desire may be permitted to feast till it dies of satiety, or kept hungry till starvation makes an end of it; affection will perish from being many times wounded. But no emotion of any magnitude can be killed by one pang.

Fourteen

■ ■ ■

The one charm of marriage is that it makes
a life of deception absolutely necessary
for both parties.

—OSCAR WILDE, Preface, *The Picture
of Dorian Gray*, 1891

CYPRIA I have told you all that I can tell in a general way about the arts by which we can engage the attentions of men and draw them into such relationships as seem good to us. I cannot go into detail without having particular situations to analyse, and in any case you should be capable now of applying the rules for yourself.

SACCHARISSA I think I could if I were only able to memorise them.

CYPRIA It is all easy enough to remember if you have grasped the underlying principle.

SACCHARISSA Which seems to be that the thing which is against my own inclination is always the correct thing to do.

CYPRIA Come, don't be discouraged. It is hard at first, I know, but when, after a little serious practice, you have once discovered what delightful success your rigid self-restraint will achieve for you, I am sure that you will throw yourself heart and soul into further experiments.

SACCHARISSA But am I really never to let myself go, even when I am auspiciously married?

CYPRIA Oh no, not if you would be assured of holding your husband, quite apart from the possibility of your still wishing to attract other men. But then, you will not want to let yourself go when you have grown to love your art. You may rest occasionally, of course: if you have some special reason for believing your position secure, you may indulge in fairly long periods of relaxation, but as for finally discarding every artifice, and forgetting your technique—why, it is unthinkable!

SACCHARISSA What would you call a special reason for believing my position secure?

CYPRIA Well, suppose you lived in some lonely district where your husband had very few opportunities for comparing you with others, or where you obviously excelled everyone about you, then you might relinquish your weapons for the time being, I admit; but whenever you visited less isolated places with him, you would have to be doubly on guard, for his enforced seclusion with you would lend great piquancy to the charms of any other women he might meet.

SACCHARISSA Surely you rather over-estimate the danger of infidelity. Among all the married people I know, there are very few husbands whom I would seriously suspect of being unfaithful.

CYPRIA You have a pleasingly guileless mind, Saccharissa. But as a matter of fact, the likelihood of an actual breach of marriage vows was not in my thoughts when I warned you to be vigilant. It does not need that extremity to demolish your power. If you were mated to a man who silently regretted his lost liberty, who chafed day by day against his restraint, who hankered—even mutely and passively—after other women, then you would have lost your hold over him just as ignominiously as if he had given you

grounds for divorce. Innumerable wives have placed themselves in this dreary, feeble situation. Those with definitely
unfaithful husbands have a rather better time, in fact.

SACCHARISSA You mean that they have an excuse for
taking their freedom?

CYPRIA That's true, but I was really thinking that a
man who is secretly enjoying forbidden pleasures generally
tries to make up to his wife for his deception by being pleasant and generous to her, whereas a man who is discontented
at home without compensating himself abroad is liable to
become an incorrigible grumbler and a petty tyrant. If you
behave sensibly, however, you need not fear to be imposed
upon in either way.

SACCHARISSA And what is your formula for sensible
behaviour?

CYPRIA Why, that you remain as attractive as possible
physically, that you are somewhat exigent and capricious,
and never quite as much engrossed in your husband as he
would like you to be, and that you wield the sceptre unosten-
tatiously, letting your obedient slave think himself your
master. You must never wholly neglect your little beguilements—your flatteries, your cajoleries, your passion for
frivolous trifles, your unreasonableness, and above all, your
ability to tease him into jealousy. Yet don't allow his jealousy
to be of the troublesome and interfering kind. You must
accustom him to letting you divert yourself in the company
of other men without making himself objectionable.

SACCHARISSA That is asking a good deal.

CYPRIA Not if he sincerely loves and trusts you, knowing in the depths of his heart that, in spite of all caprices,

you love him too. If this is so, he will have no fear that you will commit any injurious disloyalty; he has only to learn to subdue his vanity when he sees you coquetting with others.

SACCHARISSA I dare say I must be prepared to do as much for him if he should make the same demands on my forbearance.

CYPRIA Ah, I am afraid you cannot grant him quite so much latitude. You have to consider appearances. You see, if you are known to indulge in flirtations, your acquaintances will say: "Isn't she lucky? Her husband allows her to do anything she likes." But if he goes about with other women, no one remarks that his wife *allows* him to. Everyone simply pities you for being neglected by your husband, and that is more than a woman can bear.

SACCHARISSA Don't you think, Cypria, that the flirtations a married woman can safely enter into are so limited in their prospects as to be hardly worth the effort?

CYPRIA Not at all. They are desirable if only as a means of keeping her husband alert and herself fresh and youthful, and the effort is very salutary. Even the best-intentioned woman is inclined to grow a little slack in her looks, her dress and her manner of living, if there is never more than one man to notice her, and that one already bound to her. To remain lovely is an exacting business. From time to time she may surely be allowed some new inducement to enable her to bear the hardships involved in keeping slender and abreast of the fashions. It would be so much easier to become bovine and lose her husband. Then, when she found she *was* losing him, she would grow worried and irritable, and make everyone about her miserable.

To know the right woman is a liberal education.

—Elbert Hubbard,
*The Roycroft Dictionary and
Book of Epigrams,* 1923

Do you know, I'm beginning to believe that a wife *ought* to gather together a little circle of admirers in order to ensure the happiness of her home. It's positively altruistic!

SACCHARISSA You are joking now.

CYPRIA Well, perhaps I am, but there's a grain of truth in the jest.

SACCHARISSA I suppose you would never pause to consider the men whose feelings are to be played upon for the diversion of this married woman?

CYPRIA My dearest Saccharissa, after all the trouble I have taken with you, how can you be so naïve? I will not even ask you why such an unfortunate, handicapped creature as a woman should be expected to consider the feelings of the sex which has her at a disadvantage: I will merely put it to you that the men who take part in the flirtations we are discussing may derive easily as much pleasure and benefit from them as the woman. It is still true that a charming, intelligent woman may often prove a more valuable companion for a young man after she is married than she ever could have been in the days of her unsophisticated girlhood.[1] And as she cannot be suspected of matrimonial designs upon him, he need not feel self-conscious and uneasy on that subject, as most of our poverty-stricken modern youths are when they begin to flirt with an eligible girl.

SACCHARISSA Oh, I will not deny that the married women probably have better chances of alluring men than we have, but I cannot help asking—is it right for them to avail themselves of their opportunities? Some horrid married female may at this very moment be infatuating a young man whom I should like for myself.

■

[1] *It is still true* . . .

An innocent dalliance between a married woman and a young admirer was a commonplace in the annals of courtly love. While actual adultery was punishable by death, flirtations were a game, serious yet playful.

In contrast, modern marriages may seem prudish and restrictive, with conjugal vows marking the end, not the beginning, of romance. Married couples are typically portrayed as longing for the spontaneity and vitality of a new affair. Men indulge in the obligatory office fling or mid-life crisis, but women, at least those who stay home, brood over the beaux of yesteryear. Such marriages can seem almost sordid in comparison with the chaste intrigues of twelfth-century Provence.

CYPRIA She is only preparing him for you—educating him, making him less callow.

SACCHARISSA But I would rather educate him myself.

CYPRIA A thankless task! Still, if you want him so badly—this imaginary young man—bestir yourself and get him! When you honestly think you have a better and fairer claim to a lover than the woman who has won him, you are justified in making an attempt to wrest the prize away from her. A stealthy struggle, of course; no other would serve your purpose.

SACCHARISSA Your advice is inspiriting. If I should happen to see a congenial young man acting as *cavaliere servente* to a married woman, I believe I shall set myself up as her rival there and then.

CYPRIA I flatter myself that, while you bear in mind my counsels and exercise your faculty of discrimination, success is absolutely certain to be yours. You will be wise, however, to confine yourself at first to men who have already had some education—amatory, I mean—before your advent. The ingenuous stripling is difficult for a novice to manage.

SACCHARISSA I should have thought just the contrary.

CYPRIA No, he is easy enough to capture, but very hard to keep. The emotions of a youth are liable to violent reactions, and they fluctuate in the most extraordinary manner. Only an expert can cope with them, and even she may often be defeated. You have no sooner toned down the shrillness of adolescence, eliminated its gaucheries, and brought your eighteen- or nineteen-year-old wooer's attentions up to the standard you require, than he goes and practices what you have taught him upon some other woman, and she reaps the benefit of all your labour.

SACCHARISSA It is true that few men seem to have remained in love with the women who first captivated them. At what age do you think a young man may be made the partner of a love affair with reasonable hopes of long duration?

CYPRIA Certainly not before he is twenty, if so soon— unless you are in such an invulnerable position that you can afford to risk failures. A woman with a husband who fondly dotes on her, and three or four other adorers, may dabble in experiments which would be dangerous for anyone less fortunate.

SACCHARISSA If less than twenty is too young, what age is too old?

CYPRIA That must naturally depend upon your age at the time. If you are twenty, for instance, then a man of fifty is far too old for you, but if you are forty, it is an excellent age. Such things are always relative.

SACCHARISSA Do you think a woman should ever marry a man who is younger than herself?[2]

CYPRIA Why not? I cannot see the slightest objection to it. The convention by which an older husband is preferred belongs to times when women aged much sooner than men. I seriously think that the situation is reversed today. Looking about among my own acquaintance, I see women everywhere keeping their youth far better than their husbands and brothers. Yet I must warn you, that, as men still harbour old-fashioned and amazingly mistaken ideas on their own perennial youth and our early senility, if

■

[2]*Do you think a woman . . .*
Saccharissa's question and Cypria's flip reply ("Why not?") must have been an eye opener for older readers. Starting in 1900, the age difference between husband and wife imperceptibly began to narrow. In *The Culture of Love, Victorians to Moderns* (1992) the critic Stephen Kern compares the

ages of couples in Victorian and modern novels. The average fictional Victorian husband was only ten years older than his wife, while the modern man and woman were only four years apart. Fictional love affairs mirrored the reality. With advancements in birth control, obstetrics, general medicine, cosmetics, and nutrition, a woman of forty now looked and acted at least ten years younger than her mother had at the same age.

Cypria concludes the dialogue by reassuring readers that whereas love affairs may be "stepping-stones" to marriage, marriage need not mean the end of romance with all its escapades and deceptions.

you do become attached to one who is younger than yourself, you had better not draw his attention to the fact more than is absolutely necessary.

SACCHARISSA It is impossible, I suppose, to say at what time of life a woman should abandon all designs on men?

CYPRIA I imagine that if she were discreet enough always to aim at pleasing men of virtually her own age, she could go on doing so exactly as long as she wished. Nevertheless, do not let this knowledge encourage you to waste your youth. It is a terrible thing to look back on a mis-spent youth—a time when one might have been admired, courted, and beloved, and when instead one has lived a life of insipid, humdrum obscurity. What could be more reprehensible in a woman?

SACCHARISSA Cypria, I feel a glow of self-confidence, and I am eager to become guileful. Am I completely furnished for a career of wiliness? Have you no more recommendations for me?

CYPRIA No more. In your hands, Saccharissa, I have placed all the contrivances my pen can impart for heightening your natural attractions, and rendering you fit to compensate yourself for the advantages with which man is born, and which you lack. Whether, after obtaining skill by practice and judgment by experience, you turn your attention to the enviable marriage which your superior talents will enable you to make, settling down, prosperous and tranquil, to almost certain happiness, or whether you merely act upon my counsels for the light purposes of enjoying the gallantries and adulation of amiable men, you will earn success if you are earnestly bent upon it, and are willing, like a true artist, to sacrifice yourself sometimes for the sake of your art.

SACCHARISSA I will put your precepts to the proof.

CYPRIA Test them, I beg, at the first opportunity, and allow me to offer you, ever dearest Saccharissa, my most disinterested felicitations upon your glowing prospects.

Epilogue

■ ■ ■

In *Pleasure: A Discursive Guide Book,* the author, now twenty-five years older, adds a "belated postscript to her former writings":

> I should say that love is the kind of warfare in which victory is to the weak. The strong who force themselves to sell bliss for despair are the defeated. The probability is that they will not be able to keep up their self-denying resolutions. While emotions are still vigorous and clamant, that "clean break" which the inexperienced believe in so passionately is the most futile of aims; and even in the rare instances where it can be achieved, it exacts much more in the long run from the renouncer than the renounced.

■ ■ ■

About the Author

...

Discovering one of Doris Langley Moore's books is like finding a message in a bottle. Her voice, rescued from obscurity, speaks out, to use Keats's phrase, both loud and clear. Biographer, novelist, museum founder, fashion designer for film and theater, television commentator, her life was eclectic, filled with English professors and movie stars. Yet she was also that rarity, a "lady scholar," a gifted amateur who became a recognized authority on the poet Byron and the history of costume.

Born in Liverpool in 1902 to a former actress and a journalist, Doris Langley Levy grew up in South Africa, where her father was the editor of the *Sunday Times* in Johannesburg. She recalled her upbringing as a blend of music halls and museums.

At nineteen she moved to London, where she was befriended by George Bernard Shaw and the Egyptologist Sir Wallis Budge, who offered her half his fortune if she would have dinner with him once a week. (She declined.) She published her first book in 1926, a verse translation of the *Odes* of Anacreon, a fifth-century B.C. Greek poet. Around this time she married Robert Sugden Moore and moved to Yorkshire. Little is known about the marriage, except that it produced a daughter named Pandora. In an autobiographical sketch written in middle age, Moore noted tersely that after the war her marriage "dissolved."

She dated her mania for collecting costumes back to Christmas Day, 1928. During a game of Charades, her hostess gave her a period costume—a tight dress—and, surprised when Moore could fit into it, promptly let her keep it. The dress was the first in what would become the largest costume collection in the world.

Her hobby soon became a hobbyhorse, which, she once said, threatened to gallop away with her. For Moore, collecting was a blood sport to be pursued with relentless— and sometimes ruthless—zeal: She would, she claimed, do almost anything to bag a perfect specimen, whether a nineteenth-century petticoat or an evening gown by Worth.

> I think there's no method short of felony that I haven't practised. To obtain a single small item such as a pair of shoes has often cost the exchange of half a dozen letters, while some of the more extensive purchases have called for quite elaborate journeys, as well as letters, trunk calls, and, ultimately, arrangements for transport.

In Red Cross shops, junk stores, and jumble sales she picked up feminine ephemera: garters, stockings, combs, handkerchiefs, purses, fans, corsets, cravats. She possessed what art dealers call "the eye" and could discern the dowdy from the chic even in a garment over three hundred years old.

By the 1940s Moore was a recognized expert on costume and had written six books on the subject. One, *The Woman in Fashion* (1949), contains a photograph of a demure Vanessa Redgrave, age eleven, clad in a lawn dress and straw hat, the picture of the stylish young lady of 1815. In the 1950s Moore hosted a show on the subject using specimens from her own collection.

Financial difficulties after the war forced Moore to put her knowledge of fashion to good use. She worked in films and theater, writing scripts and designing costumes, most notably the versatile white suit and hat that Katharine Hepburn wears throughout *The African Queen*. In her memoir, *The Making Of "The African Queen,"* Hepburn remembers defying the director John Huston by insisting on Moore: "I told him I didn't want his woman; I wanted Langley Moore and I would go see what she had in the museum. Also, she had been born in Africa and knew of missionaries from a grandparent who was one." Her innacuracy about Moore's birth nothwithstanding, Hepburn was fascinated by the collection—especially Queen Victoria's underpants with their fifty-inch waistline. Some ten years later Moore designed the costumes for *Freud*, another Huston film. She also wrote a scenario for a ballet, *The Quest*, danced by Margot Fonteyn, who became a close friend.

In the 1940s, when the study of fashion was dismissed as frivolous, Moore decided to establish a museum of costume—the first of its kind in the world. In 1963, after several false starts, her collection found a permanent home in the newly restored Assembly Rooms at Bath. The Museum of Costume was actually a Museum of Fashion—in other words, frumpy, ceremonial, and native dresses were excluded from the display. The rule was broken for such sartorial luminaries as the dashing Albanian costume that Byron wore in the famous Thomas Philips portrait in the National Portrait Gallery, and the desert garb worn by Lawrence of Arabia.

But when the Council moved the collection from the ground floor to what she considered the ignominy of the basement, Moore resigned as Honorary Advisor to the Museum. Incensed at their philistinism, she never forgave the Council, viewing it with the disdain she later reserved for the "Thatcher crowd." She would never see her collection again.

The last twenty-five years of Moore's life were given over to what can only be called Byronmania. In *The Technique,* Moore warned her readers never to reclaim a rake, yet she spent the last years of her life doing just that. In her three books about the poet and his family, the *enfant terrible* of English literature is transformed into a man more sinned against than sinning. His faults are explained, his vices turned to virtues. She studied Byron not with the detachment of a scholar but with the ardor of a mistress. She once said, "I was perhaps the only woman to whom nothing but pleasure has come from loving that poet." A letter she wrote to the *Times* in Byron's defense prompted the poet's great-great-granddaughter to open the family vault, a vast, uncatalogued trove of private papers. Moore was the first scholar to examine and write about primary materials that would become the basis for virtually every biography written on the poet. Thus, in Byron studies at least, Moore's place is secure.

Apart from her works on Byron and fashion, Moore wrote six novels, two biographies (E. Nesbit, Marie Bashkirtseff), four works of nonfiction (including *Pleasure: A Discursive Guide Book*), and two plays. She was a founding member of the Costume Society and the Byron Society in Great Britain and a Fellow of the Royal Society of Literature. She received the OBE in 1971.

Moore was never afraid to challenge the shibboleths and creeds of the age. She became an authority on fashion when the subject wasn't fashionable, and she dared to challenge traditional Byron scholars. *The Vulgar Heart: An Enquiry into the Sentimental Tendencies of Public Opinion* (1945), her scathing critique on conventional pieties such as patriotism and motherhood, seems progressive even by today's standards. In her diverse life, one philosophy emerges: her belief that the pursuit of pleasure is serious business and that joy should be cultivated, not curbed. She denounced "puritans," a generic term she applied to the "pleasure-fearing" who value hardship for its own sake. Creature comforts, not cold virtue, make for a well-lived life. In *Pleasure* she confesses:

I have always let friendship lapse into well-wishing acquaintainceship when there is a failure to observe that certain things should be hot—as tea, coffee, curry, most dinner plates, sitting room fires, heating pipes in winter, and especially bath-water.

But it was the "luxuries of the mind" she valued most: dance, opera, the visual arts—even daydreaming.

Doris Langley Moore had the rare ability to perceive what was profound and enduring in the ostensibly trivial. In the caprices of fashion she saw "the sign of a romantic spirit which triumphs over utilitarian considerations." Indeed, in old age, a time when most turn to the contemplation of eternity, she still delighted in ephemera. In her obituary in the *Guardian*, William St. Clair wrote: "Though she hated the inconveniences of old age, she never lost the defiantly frivolous and flirtatious attitude toward life that she shared with her poet. The last time I saw her in hospital she was studying the summer fashions."

N.E.

■ ■ ■